Level 2 • Part 2

Integrated Chinese

中文听说读写
中文聽説讀寫

WORKBOOK Simplified and Traditional Characters

Third Edition

THIRD EDITION BY

Yuehua Liu and Tao-chung Yao
Liangyan Ge, Yaohua Shi, Nyan-Ping Bi

ORIGINAL EDITION BY

Yuehua Liu and Tao-chung Yao
Nyan-Ping Bi and Yaohua Shi

CHENG & TSUI
BOSTON

21 20 19 18 17 16   5 6 7 8 9 10
5th Printing

Published by
Cheng & Tsui Company, Inc.
25 West Street
Boston, MA 02111-1213 USA
Fax (617) 426-3669
chengtsui.co
"Bringing Asia to the World"™

ISBN 978-0-88727-692-7

Cover Design: studioradia.com

Cover Photographs: Man with map © Getty Images; Shanghai skyline © David Pedre/iStockphoto; Building with masks © Wu Jie; Night market © Andrew Buko. Used by permission.

Interior Design: Wanda España, Wee Design
Illustrations: Eloise Narrigan, www.eloisedraws.com
Selected Illustrations (p. 9, 47, 48, 64, 107, 108, 124, 143): 洋洋兔动漫
Editing: Kristen Wanner, Zheng-sheng Zhang, Minying Tan, Laurel Damashek
Project Management: Laurel Damashek
Production: Victoria E. Kichuk
Manufacturing: JoAnne Sweeney
Proofreading: Victoria E. Kichuk, Laurel Damashek
Composition: Charlesworth
Printing and Binding: Transcontinental

The *Integrated Chinese* series includes books, workbooks, character workbooks, audio products, multimedia products, teacher's resources, and more. Visit chengtsui.co for more information on the other components of *Integrated Chinese*.

Printed in the United States of America.

Contents

Preface v

Lesson 11: 中國的節日/中国的节日 1
Chinese Festivals
    I. Listening Comprehension... 1
    II. Speaking Exercises 2
    III. Reading Comprehension 3
    IV. Writing and Grammar Exercises 8

Lesson 12: 中國的變化/中国的变化 19
Changes in China
    I. Listening Comprehension... 19
    II. Speaking Exercises 20
    III. Reading Comprehension 21
    IV. Writing and Grammar Exercises 27

Lesson 13: 旅遊/旅游 35
Travel
    I. Listening Comprehension... 35
    II. Speaking Exercises 37
    III. Reading Comprehension 37
    IV. Writing and Grammar Exercises 44

Lesson 14: 生活與健康/生活与健康 55
Life and Wellness
    I. Listening Comprehension... 55
    II. Speaking Exercises 56
    III. Reading Comprehension 57
    IV. Writing and Grammar Exercises 62

Lesson 15: 男女平等 73
Gender Equality
    I. Listening Comprehension... 73
    II. Speaking Exercises 74
    III. Reading Comprehension 75
    IV. Writing and Grammar Exercises 79

Let's Review! (Lessons 11–15) 89

Lesson 16: 環境保護與節約能源/环境保护与节约能源 97
Environmental Protection and Energy Conservation
    I. Listening Comprehension 97
    II. Speaking Exercises 98
    III. Reading Comprehension 99
    IV. Writing and Grammar Exercises 106

Lesson 17: 理財與投資/理财与投资 115
Money Management and Investing
    I. Listening Comprehension 115
    II. Speaking Exercises 117
    III. Reading Comprehension 117
    IV. Writing and Grammar Exercises 123

Lesson 18: 中國歷史/中国历史 131
Chinese History
    I. Listening Comprehension 131
    II. Speaking Exercises 133
    III. Reading Comprehension 133
    IV. Writing and Grammar Exercises 139

Lesson 19: 面試/面试 149
Interviewing for a Job
    I. Listening Comprehension 149
    II. Speaking Exercises 151
    III. Reading Comprehension 151
    IV. Writing and Grammar Exercises 157

Lesson 20: 外國人在中國/外国人在中国 167
Foreigners in China
    I. Listening Comprehension 167
    II. Speaking Exercises 168
    III. Reading Comprehension 169
    IV. Writing and Grammar Exercises 174

Let's Review! (Lessons 16–20) 183

Preface

This workbook accompanies the third edition of *Integrated Chinese* (*IC*), Level 2 Part 2. The exercises cover the language form and the four language skills of listening, speaking, reading, and writing. They are arranged by language skill into four sections: Listening Comprehension, Speaking, Reading Comprehension, and Writing & Grammar. Within each section, exercises vary in difficulty in order to provide flexibility to suit different curricular needs.

These exercises are designed primarily for students to do outside of class, either as preparation before class or assignments after class. For instance, the listening comprehension questions based on the text of each lesson should be done when students are preparing for the lesson for the first time or before they read the text. The other exercises are for students to prepare at home, although some of them, particularly speaking exercises, can also be done in class. Unless otherwise indicated, all the exercises in the Writing and Grammar Exercises section should be done in Chinese. In general, teachers should assign the exercises at their discretion; they should not feel pressured into using all of them and should feel free to use them out of sequence, if appropriate. Moreover, teachers can complement this workbook with their own exercises.

We have made several improvements and added a number of new features in the third edition of the workbook.

Three Modes of Communication

Our exercises cover the three modes of communication—interpretive, interpersonal, and presentational—as explained in "Standards for Foreign Language Learning in the 21st Century." We have labeled the exercises as interpretive, interpersonal, or presentational wherever applicable. Additional resources on this topic are available at **chengtsui.co**.

Listening Rejoinders

To help students develop interpersonal skills, we have added a rejoinder to each lesson. The rejoinders are designed to improve students' ability to listen and respond to questions or remarks logically and meaningfully.

Character and Word Building Exercises

While training students to work on their proficiency at the sentence and paragraph-length levels, we realized there was a need to help students solidify their foundation in character recognition and word association. We have thus added character and word building exercises to each lesson.

New Reading Exercises

To help students understand how their newly acquired vocabulary and grammatical structures function in meaningful contexts and, at the same time, to avoid overwhelming students with extra materials containing words they haven't learned, we have added newly composed reading exercises and deleted the ancient Chinese parables that were included in previous editions. These parables, however, are now available online at **chengtsui.co**. Students should be encouraged to use them as supplementary reading materials with the help of a dictionary.

More Authentic Materials

To build a bridge between the pedagogical materials used in the classroom and the materials that students will encounter in the target language environment, we have added more authentic materials such as signs, posters, advertisements, and other documents in the exercises for all lessons.

New Illustrations

To make the exercises more interesting and appealing, we have added many illustrations to the exercises. These visual images increase the variety of exercise types, and also encourage students to answer questions directly in Chinese without going through the translation process.

Contextualized Grammar Exercises and Task-Oriented Assignments

The ultimate goal of learning any language is to be able to communicate in that language. With this goal in mind, we pay equal attention to language form and language function, and have created task-based exercises to train students to handle real-life situations using the language accurately and appropriately. We have rewritten many items, especially in the translation section, to provide linguistic context and to reflect the language used in real life.

Learner-Centered Tasks

We believe that the exercises in the workbook should not only integrate the content of the textbook, but also relate to student life. We include exercises that simulate daily life with topics and themes that students can easily relate to. We hope these exercises will actively engage students in the subject matter and keep them interested in the language-learning process. Since the world is constantly changing, we also have tried to add exercises that will train students to meet the needs of today's world, such as writing e-mail messages in Chinese.

Storytelling Exercises

To coach students to describe what they see and use their language skills to construct narratives, we have added one storytelling exercise to each lesson. This exercise is designed to help students develop skills for organizing ideas and presenting them in a coherent manner. It also provides practice in using transitional elements and cohesive devices to make the story progress smoothly and logically. This exercise is suitable for either speaking or writing. The teacher can ask students to submit the story as a written exercise and/or ask them to make an oral presentation in class.

New Review Exercises

At the end of every five lessons, a cumulative review unit is available to those students who wish to do a periodic progress check. These units are flexible, short, and useful as a review tool. They include exercises that reinforce a variety of language skills, from practicing pronunciation to recalling vocabulary and writing cohesive narratives. Since the review units do not introduce any new learning topics, they can be included in the teaching plan at the teacher's discretion.

Acknowledgments

We would like to take this opportunity to thank all those who have given us feedback in the past, and extend our sincere gratitude to Professor Zheng-sheng Zhang of San Diego State University and to Ms. Kristen Wanner for their invaluable editorial comments and to Ms. Laurel Damashek and Ms. Minying Tan at Cheng & Tsui for their support throughout the editorial and production process. We welcome your comments and feedback; please send any observations or suggestions to **editor@cheng-tsui.com.**

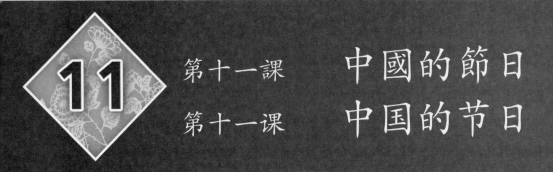

第十一課　　中國的節日
第十一课　　中国的节日

🔘 I. Listening Comprehension

A. Textbook Content (INTERPRETIVE)

Listen to the recording for the Textbook and answer the questions in English.

1. How would you describe the apartment and area in which Xuemei's uncle and aunt live?

_____

2. Why did Xuemei's aunt decide to prepare the Chinese New Year's Eve dinner at home, instead of going to a restaurant?

_____

3. What dish does Xuemei say is essential for a Chinese New Year's Eve dinner, and why?

_____

4. Besides Chinese New Year, what other major traditional Chinese festivals do the characters in the dialogue mention at the dinner table?

_____

5. What New Year gifts do Xuemei and Ke Lin receive from Xuemei's uncle and aunt?

_____

6. To whom does Xuemei send Chinese New Year's greetings after dinner?

_____

B. Workbook Dialogue (INTERPRETIVE)

Listen to the recording for the Workbook and answer the questions.

Questions (True/False):

( )　**1.**　The speakers have lived in their current residence for less than a year.

( )　**2.**　The conversation most likely takes place at the dinner table.

( )　**3.**　The man likes not only their residence but also their neighborhood.

( )　**4.**　The woman thinks that their residence is not completely furnished yet.

( )　**5.**　The speakers are happy to be without children.

( )　**6.**　The speakers make a toast using tea.

C. Workbook Narratives (INTERPRETIVE)

Listen to the recording for the Workbook and answer the questions in English.

1. Questions:

a. What is the purpose of this voicemail?

_____

b. Has Little Jiang been in China for many years? How do you know?

_____

c. What did Little Jiang like best about the Chinese New Year?

_____

d. What other missing information does Little Jiang expect from Little Lin next time?

_____

2. Questions:

a. Does Old Wang live in Sichuan, Beijing, or elsewhere? How do you know?

_____

b. Did Old Wang and Mrs. Wang try to book a dinner reservation for their New Year's Eve dinner at a restaurant? Why or why not?

_____

c. Did the Wangs have their New Year's Eve dinner at home or at a restaurant? Why?

_____

d. Why did Little Wang want to go against tradition and not light firecrackers?

_____

D. Workbook Listening Rejoinder (INTERPERSONAL)

In this section, you will hear two people talking. After hearing the first speaker, select the best from the four possible responses given by the second speaker.

_____

II. Speaking Exercises

A. Practice asking and answering the following questions. (INTERPERSONAL)

1. 你住校內還是校外?

你住校内还是校外?

2. 幾房幾廳幾衛?

几房几厅几卫?

3. 環境怎麼樣？住起來舒服不舒服？

　　环境怎么样？住起来舒服不舒服？

4. 除夕是哪一天？

5. 今年過什麼節，你會回家跟家人團圓？

　　今年过什么节，你会回家跟家人团圆？

B. Practice speaking on the following topics. (PRESENTATIONAL)

1. 請談談中國人怎麼過春節。

　　请谈谈中国人怎么过春节。

2. 請談談在你的國家，人們怎麼過新年。

　　请谈谈在你的国家，人们怎么过新年。

3. Review the lesson, and recap the traditional Chinese festivals, their dates, and the foods typically associated with them. Which Chinese holiday appeals to you the most, and why?

III. Reading Comprehension

A. Building Words

Complete this section by writing the characters, the *pinyin*, and the English equivalent of each new word formed. Guess the meaning before you use a dictionary to confirm.

1. "社會"的"社" + "小區"的"區"

　 "社会"的"社" + "小区"的"区"

　　　　　　　　→ _____ _____ _____

　　　　　　　　　　　　new word　　*pinyin*　　English

2. "幸福"的"福" + "氣氛"的"氣"

　 "幸福"的"福" + "气氛"的"气"

　　　　　　　　→ _____ _____ _____

3. "奇怪"的"怪" + "購物"的"物"

　 "奇怪"的"怪" + "购物"的"物"

　　　　　　　　→ _____ _____ _____

4. "月餅"的"餅" + "乾杯"的"乾"

"月饼"的"饼" + "干杯"的"干"

→ _____ _____ _____

5. "拜年"的"年" + "蛋糕"的"糕"

→ _____ _____ _____

B. The following is a conversation between a host and a guest visiting her house for the first time. Fill in the blanks with phrases provided. (INTERPRETIVE)

(TRADITIONAL)

住起來	吃起來	穿起來	喝起來	做起來

A: 您的新家環境真不錯，_____很舒服吧?

B: 還行，挺安靜的。請喝咖啡。

A: 謝謝! …您這咖啡_____特別香。您在咖啡裡放了什麼?

B: 咖啡裏什麼都沒放，_____很簡單，有空我教你。來，吃點兒月餅。

A: 您的月餅_____真香，肯定很貴吧?

B: 我也不清楚，是朋友送的。我今天穿的這件衣服，也是同一個朋友送的。

A: 您的朋友真會買東西。這件衣服，您_____特別好看。

(SIMPLIFIED)

住起来	吃起来	穿起来	喝起来	做起来

A: 您的新家环境真不错，_____很舒服吧?

B: 还行，挺安静的。请喝咖啡。

A: 谢谢! …您这咖啡_____特别香。您在咖啡里放了什么?

B: 咖啡里什么都没放，_____很简单，有空我教你。来，吃点儿月饼。

A: 您的月饼_____真香，肯定很贵吧？

B: 我也不清楚，是朋友送的。我今天穿的这件衣服，也是同一个朋友送的。

A: 您的朋友真会买东西。这件衣服，您_____特别好看。

C. Read the passages and answer the questions. (INTERPRETIVE)

1.

(TRADITIONAL)

　　雪梅跟她父母的感情很好。她已經兩年沒有和爸爸媽媽一起過春節了。這次回杭州，她本來打算陪父母過年以後再去北京，可是舅舅從北京打電話說有一個實習的機會，馬上就要開始工作。爸爸媽媽也說，這個機會對雪梅的事業太重要了。於是雪梅和柯林春節前就到了北京。雪梅在北京給媽媽打電話說，她和柯林已經在杭州一家有名的餐館給爸爸媽媽和弟弟訂好了年夜飯，這樣媽媽就不用花時間準備了。可是媽媽說，到餐館訂餐方便是方便，可是不如在家裏吃年夜飯有家庭氣氛。雪梅覺得媽媽說得有道理，於是就打電話告訴那家餐館不訂餐了。

(SIMPLIFIED)

　　雪梅跟她父母的感情很好。她已经两年没有和爸爸妈妈一起过春节了。这次回杭州，她本来打算陪父母过年以后再去北京，可是舅舅从北京打电话说有一个实习的机会，马上就要开始工作。爸爸妈妈也说，这个机会对雪梅的事业太重要了。于是雪梅和柯林春节前就到了北京。雪梅在北京给妈妈打电话说，她和柯林已经在杭州一家有名的餐馆给爸爸妈妈和弟弟订好了年夜饭，这样妈妈就不用花时间准备了。可是妈妈说，到餐馆订餐方便是方便，可是不如在家里吃年夜饭有家庭气氛。雪梅觉得妈妈说得有道理，于是就打电话告诉那家餐馆不订餐了。

Questions (True/False):

( ) **1.** Xuemei went to Beijing earlier than she had originally planned.

( ) **2.** Xuemei feels bad that she had spent only one Spring Festival with her parents in the last two years.

( ) **3.** Xuemei had intended to cook the New Year's Eve dinner for her family.

( ) **4.** Xuemei's parents and brother will most likely have their New Year's Eve dinner at home.

Questions (Multiple Choice):

( ) **5.** Xuemei's parents persuaded Xuemei to leave for Beijing before the Spring Festival because _____.

    a. they thought Xuemei's uncle would need her company in Beijing

    b. they knew Xuemei would find a better job in Beijing

    c. they knew the internship would be important for her future career

( ) **6.** Xuemei finally agrees with her mother's arrangement for the New Year's Eve dinner because it is _____.

    a. less expensive

    b. more casual and cozier

    c. easier

2.

(TRADITIONAL)

在中國，很多人在過春節的時候都說吉利 (jílì: auspicious) 的話，可是有時候說吉利的話不太容易。有一位王先生，家裏的家俱都很新很漂亮，他覺得過年應該在牆上貼兩張畫才有節日的氣氛。他貼好了第一張，想把第二張貼得跟第一張一樣高，就對十歲的兒子說："你幫我看看，要是我把畫貼得太高了，你就說'發財'；要是太低了，你就說'健康'"。說著，王先生就把第二張畫貼到牆上了，貼得正好，不比第一張高，也不比第一張低。這時候兒子高興地說："爸爸，你太棒了，不發財，也不健康。"

(SIMPLIFIED)

在中国，很多人在过春节的时候都说吉利 (jílì: auspicious) 的话，可是有时候说吉利的话不太容易。有一位王先生，家里的家具都很新很漂亮，他觉得过年应该在墙上贴两张画才有节日的气氛。他贴好了第一张，想把第二张贴得跟第一张一样高，就对十岁的儿子说："你帮我看看，要是我把画贴得太高了，你就说'发财'；要是太低了，你就说'健康'"。说着，王先生就把第二张画贴到墙上了，贴得正好，不比第一张高，也不比第一张低。这时候儿子高兴地说："爸爸，你太棒了，不发财，也不健康。"

Questions (True/False):

( ) **1.** According to the passage, it is not always easy to say auspicious things.

( ) **2.** Mr. Wang thinks that a couple of pictures on the wall will increase the festive atmosphere.

( ) **3.** Of Mr. Wang's two pictures, the first has to do with wealth and the second has to do with health.

( ) **4.** Mr. Wang tries to make his son say auspicious words.

( ) **5.** Mr. Wang's son is glad that his father has been able to position the pictures perfectly.

( ) **6.** The son knows that his father will have neither wealth nor health.

D. Look at the ad below and list in English the things that you like and don't like about the place. Before calling the landlord, jot down in Chinese some of the questions you may want to ask. (INTERPRETIVE/PRESENTATIONAL)

出租二居室

出租本小區二居室,室內非常乾淨，環境好，有空調，有電視，冰箱，洗衣機，雙人床，寫字桌，希望你愛乾淨，如果你有意租房，就給我打電話吧．

聯繫人：徐先生 137182XXXXX

出租二居室

出租本小区二居室,室内非常干净，环境好，有空调，有电视，冰箱，洗衣机，双人床，写字桌，希望你爱干净，如果你有意租房，就给我打电话吧。

联系人：徐先生 137182XXXXX

(二居室＝兩個臥室/两个卧室)

Likes:	Dislikes:
_____	_____
_____	_____
_____	_____

Questions:

_____   _____

_____   _____

_____   _____

IV. Writing and Grammar Exercises

A. Building Characters

Form a character by combining the given components as instructed. Then write a word, a phrase, or a short sentence in which that character appears.

1. 左邊一個人字旁，右邊一個"到"，

左边一个人字旁，右边一个"到"，

是 _____的_____ 。

2. 外邊一個"气"，裏邊一個"分鐘"的"分"，

外边一个"气"，里边一个"分钟"的"分"，

是 _____的_____ 。

3. 左邊一個"工作"的"工"，右邊一個"費力氣"的"力"，

左边一个"工作"的"工"，右边一个"费力气"的"力"，

是 _____的_____ 。

4. 左邊一個三點水，右邊一個"良好"的"良"，

左边一个三点水，右边一个"良好"的"良"，

是 _____的_____ 。

5. 左邊一個人字旁，右邊一個"專業"的"專"，

左边一个人字旁，右边一个"专业"的"专"，

是 _____的_____ 。

6. 外邊一個"口"，裏邊一個"售貨員"的"員"，

外边一个"口"，里边一个"售货员"的"员"，

是 _____的_____ 。

7. 左邊一個"貝"，右邊一個"剛才"的"才"，

　　左边一个"贝"，右边一个"刚才"的"才"，

　　是 ＿＿＿＿＿＿＿＿的＿＿＿＿＿＿ 。

8. 上邊一個"因為"的"因"，下邊一個"心事"的"心"，

　　上边一个"因为"的"因"，下边一个"心事"的"心"，

　　是 ＿＿＿＿＿＿＿＿的＿＿＿＿＿＿ 。

B. Look at the illustrations given and state what these people are busy doing.

EXAMPLE:

→　**A:** 天明呢？ 他忙什麼呢？　　　**B:** 他忙著打掃房間呢。
　　　天明呢？ 他忙什么呢？　　　　　他忙着打扫房间呢。

1.

 ＿＿＿＿＿＿＿＿＿＿＿＿＿＿＿＿＿＿＿＿＿＿＿＿＿＿＿＿＿＿＿

2.

 ＿＿＿＿＿＿＿＿＿＿＿＿＿＿＿＿＿＿＿＿＿＿＿＿＿＿＿＿＿＿＿

3.

 ＿＿＿＿＿＿＿＿＿＿＿＿＿＿＿＿＿＿＿＿＿＿＿＿＿＿＿＿＿＿＿

C. What expertise do you expect people in certain professions to have?
Use "V 得出(來)/V 得出(来)" to specify.

      EXAMPLE: a coffee taster   origin

         <u>他能喝得出(來)咖啡是從哪兒來的</u>。

         <u>他能喝得出(來)咖啡是从哪儿来的</u>。

  1. a restaurant critic   type of cuisine and authenticity

→ _____

  2. an entertainment agent   who can sing and who can dance

→ _____

  3. a language teacher   whether a student's pronunciation is good

→ _____

D. Answer the questions emphatically by using reduplicated measure words.

  1. 除夕晚上哪家餐館有位子？

      除夕晚上哪家餐馆有位子？

→ _____

  2. 柯林的同學中誰是球迷？

      柯林的同学中谁是球迷？

→ _____

  3. 麗莎哪天有中文課？

      丽莎哪天有中文课？

星期一	星期二	星期三	星期四	星期五
中文	中文	中文	中文	中文

→ _____

E. The characters in the textbook all follow their own routines and schedules. Describe their routines in Chinese based on the cues.

EXAMPLE: having soup → having (other) food

  張天明一般都先喝湯再吃飯。
  张天明一般都先喝汤再吃饭。

 1. doing homework → having dinner

→ _____

 2. tidying up living room → tidying up the bedroom

→ _____

3. looking up information online → looking up information in the library

→ _____

F. Translate the ad into Chinese. (PRESENTATIONAL)

出 租 一 居

One-bedroom apartment for rent. Close to BLCU and 10 minutes walk from subway. Tv, fridge, wash-machine, air-conditionner, microwave, bed, desk, table, sofa, tea-table and so on……。 Internet and hot water 24 hours.

Telephone number: 158016⬛⬛⬛ Joe

Note that BLCU refers to Beijing Language and Culture University

(北京語言大學/北京语言大学)

_____

G. Translate the following dialogues into Chinese. (PRESENTATIONAL)

1. **A:** What have you decided to do after the semester ends?

   B: Go to New York to do an internship and find a job.

   你党定了学膜结束了一后 想做什么呢？

   你会去组约实习,找工作。

2. **A:** Where you're from (你們那兒/你们那儿), can you set off firecrackers for the Spring Festival?

   B: No. We can't buy firecrackers, either.

   你们那儿能春节放鞭炮吗？

   不能放,也不能买。

3. **A:** What Thanksgiving traditions does your family have?

   B: My family eats together on Thanksgiving. After lunch we watch American football. On Thanksgiving it's very boisterous in my house.

   你的家人有什么感恩传统？

4. **A:** How is the environment of your residential community?

   B: The environment is very nice, very quiet. And it's very close to school, really convenient.

5. A: Where did you go for the Spring Festival?

　B: I went to Hangzhou to see my (maternal) uncle and his wife. They have a three-bedroom, one-dining room, one-living room, two-bathroom apartment. It's very comfortable (to live there).

　A: When did you get to Hangzhou?

　B: I got to Hangzhou on New Year's Eve. My uncle made a reservation at a restaurant, so we didn't have New Year's Eve dinner at home.

　A: Do your uncle and his wife cook?

　B: They like to cook very much, but they devote all their time to their careers, so they are very busy. They often don't have time to cook.

　A: What do your uncle and his wife do?

　B: My uncle is a university professor. His wife is a lawyer.

　A: Do they have children?

　B: They don't have any children. They are a two-person world. They are very fond of each other.

_____

_____

_____

_____

_____

_____

_____

_____

_____

_____

6. A: My Chinese classmate invited me to have Chinese New Year's Eve dinner at her house. I wonder (I don't know) what Chinese people have for Chinese New Year's Eve dinner.

　B: If your classmate's family is from the North, they'll definitely have dumplings.

　A: Great! I like eating dumplings. What else?

　B: Also Chinese people must have fish for Chinese New Year's Eve dinner. Furthermore you can't eat it all. You have to leave some on the plate.

　A: Why? Isn't that wasteful?

B: Because "fish" is pronounced the same as "surplus," in other words, "leaving some behind."

A: How interesting! Thank you for telling me. Otherwise, I'd probably eat the whole fish.

_____

_____

_____

_____

_____

_____

_____

_____

H. Translate the following passage into Chinese. (PRESENTATIONAL)

China has many traditional holidays. Besides the Spring Festival, there are also the Lantern Festival, the Dragon Boat Festival, the Mid-Autumn Festival, and the Qingming Festival. Every year, the fifteenth day of the first month on the lunar calendar is the Lantern Festival. On that day, Chinese people eat dumplings made of glutinous rice. The fifth day of the fifth month of the lunar calendar is the Dragon Boat Festival. Every Chinese family eats *zongzi*. The fifteenth day of the eighth month of the lunar calendar is the Mid-Autumn Festival, which is a day of family reunion—a bit like America's Thanksgiving. Everyone has to eat moon cakes to celebrate the Mid-Autumn Festival. April 5th is the Qingming Festival (清明節/清明节), which is also an important traditional holiday.

_____

_____

_____

_____

_____

_____

_____

I. It's that time of the year again: time to call, text-message, email, or write a card to your Chinese friends and their families to wish them a happy Chinese New Year. Make sure your New Year wishes are appropriate based on your relationship with the recipient. Fill in the table of the recipients, how you will communicate with them, and your wishes for each of them. (PRESENTATIONAL)

Name	Mode of Communication	Wishes
Person 1: 中文老師/中文老师	寫卡片/写卡片	
Person 2:		
Person 3:		
Person 4:		
Person 5:		
Person 6:		

For those whom you plan to call on the phone, rehearse with a partner or record a message for your teacher.

For those to whom you plan to write a letter or email, write your message here.

J. Find two or three photos of a Chinese holiday by searching online or asking friends and family. Use Chinese to write a brief news article or a letter to a friend describing the pictures. Make sure to describe the atmosphere, what people are doing and eating, how the places are decorated, etc. You can use your imagination to make up quotes from the people celebrating the festival. Use at least two of the grammar patterns and five new words and phrases from this lesson. (PRESENTATIONAL)

K. This year, you will be starting a new tradition by hosting a Chinese New Year celebration for your family. Write a letter to your family members describing how they can help decorate and cook for the holiday, what they should expect to do, what they should wear, what they should bring, etc. The more you teach them about the holiday, the more fun it will be! Use at least three of the grammar patterns or words and phrases from this lesson (PRESENTATIONAL).

L. Storytelling (PRESENTATIONAL)

Write a story in Chinese based on the four cartoons below. Make sure that your story has a beginning, a middle, and an end. Also make sure that the transition from one picture to the next is smooth and logical.

1

2

3

4

第十二课　中國的變化
第十二课　中国的变化

🔘 I. Listening Comprehension

A. Textbook Content (INTERPRETIVE)

Listen to the recording for the Textbook and answer the questions in English.

1. Are Tianming and Lisa returning to the United States right after their visit to Nanjing? Why or why not?

_____

2. What did Tianming's father want Tianming to do in Nanjing? Does Tianming accomplish that mission?

_____

3. What is Tianming's impression of Nanjing?

_____

4. According to the characters, what changes have taken place in Nanjing?

_____

5. According to Tianming's cousin, which part of the city is most distinctly Chinese?

_____

B. Workbook Dialogue (INTERPRETIVE)

Listen to the recording for the Workbook and answer the questions.

Questions (True/False):

(　) **1.** Both the man and the woman have been away from this place for some time.

(　) **2.** The speakers find themselves in a very quiet environment.

(　) **3.** The restaurant has expanded its business in recent years.

(　) **4.** The parking lot in front of the restaurant is full of cars and bicycles.

(　) **5.** Over the years, the restaurant has not made many changes to its menu.

(　) **6.** The current customers of the restaurant like the same types of food that people of the older generation preferred.

C. Workbook Narratives (INTERPRETIVE)

Listen to the recording for the Workbook and answer the questions in English.

1. Questions:

a. Did Mr. Qian go to college in Beijing? How do you know?

_____

b. Did Mr. Qian find any places in Hangzhou that he was familiar with?

_____

c. Was Mr. Qian happy about the drastic changes to his hometown? Why or why not?

_____

2. Questions:

a. How does the speaker describe the old Nanjing that he knew?

_____

b. According to the speaker, how has Nanjing changed?

_____

c. What was the speaker's impression of Nanjing when she went there last month?

_____

d. How would you describe the speaker's attitude toward the changes in Nanjing?

_____

D. Workbook Listening Rejoinder (INTERPERSONAL)

In this section, you will hear two people talking. After hearing the first speaker, select the best from the four possible responses given by the second speaker.

_____

II. Speaking Exercises

A. Practice asking and answering the following questions. (INTERPERSONAL)

1. 你坐過高速火車嗎？坐過幾次？從哪兒坐到哪兒？

你坐过高速火车吗？坐过几次？从哪儿坐到哪儿？

2. 你喜歡住在安靜的城市還是熱鬧的城市？為什麼？

你喜欢住在安静的城市还是热闹的城市？为什么？

3. 你的城市新蓋的高樓多還是傳統的建築多？你喜歡住在新蓋的高樓
裏還是傳統的建築裏？為什麼？

你的城市新盖的高楼多还是传统的建筑多？你喜欢住在新盖的高楼
里还是传统的建筑里？为什么？

4. 你遊覽過哪些城市？對哪個城市的印象最好？為什麼？

你游览过哪些城市？对哪个城市的印象最好？为什么？

B. Practice speaking on the following topics. (PRESENTATIONAL)

1. 請談談你的老家有什麼特色。

请谈谈你的老家有什么特色。

2. 請談談你的老家最近有些什麼變化。

请谈谈你的老家最近有些什么变化。

3. Review the lesson, and have a conversation with your partner about your favorite cities.
Do you prefer places with traditional characteristics or modern excitement, cities with
popular tourist sites or convenient shopping centers?

III. Reading Comprehension

A. Building Words

Complete this section by writing the characters, the *pinyin*, and the English equivalent of each new
word formed. Guess the meaning before you use a dictionary to confirm.

1. "綠色" 的 "綠" ＋ "變化" 的 "化"

"绿色" 的 "绿" ＋ "变化" 的 "化"

→ _____　_____　_____

new word　　　　*pinyin*　　　　English

2. "上班" 的 "班" ＋ "公共汽車" 的 "車"

"上班" 的 "班" ＋ "公共汽车" 的 "车"

→ _____　_____　_____

3. "一座山" 的 "座" ＋ "位子" 的 "位"

→ _____　_____　_____

4. "回來"的"回"+"聲音"的"聲"

"回来"的"回"+"声音"的"声"

→ _____ _____ _____

5. "農村"的"農"+"民以食為天"的"民"

"农村"的"农"+"民以食为天"的"民"

→ _____ _____ _____

B. The following is a conversation between two friends. Fill in the blanks with phrases provided. (INTERPRETIVE)

(TRADITIONAL)

的確	儘可能	看來	竟	完全	可	從來

A: 元宵節快到了，咱們做點元宵吃，怎麼樣?

B: 做元宵? 我_____不行，_____沒做過。

A: 你在中國出生、長大的，_____沒做過元宵?

B: 我最不喜歡進廚房，能不做菜就_____不做菜。別說做元宵了，我連一般的菜都不太會做。

A: _____這次做元宵得_____靠我了。

B: 沒錯，_____得靠你。

(SIMPLIFIED)

的确	尽可能	看来	竟	完全	可	从来

A: 元宵节快到了，咱们做点元宵吃，怎么样?

B: 做元宵? 我_____不行，_____没做过。

A: 你在中国出生、长大的，_____没做过元宵?

B: 我最不喜欢进厨房，能不做菜就_____不做菜。别说做元宵了，我连一般的菜都不太会做。

A: _____这次做元宵得_____靠我了。

B: 没错，_____得靠你。

C. Match the sentences on the left with the replies on the right.

1. 請問，我明天什麼時候來上班？ 请问，我明天什么时候来上班？	**a.** 別着急，我們儘可能幫你找。 别着急，我们尽可能帮你找。
2. 糟糕，我的電腦丟了。 糟糕，我的电脑丢了。	**b.** 出去旅行應該儘可能少帶東西。 出去旅行应该尽可能少带东西。
3. 等等我，我行李還沒有整理好。 等等我，我行李还没有整理好。	**c.** 請儘可能早點來。 请尽可能早点来。
4. 我們怎麼讓更多的遊客來我們 這兒旅遊呢？ 我们怎么让更多的游客来我们 这儿旅游呢？	**d.** 儘可能保留有特色的傳統建築。 尽可能保留有特色的传统建筑。

D. Read the passages and answer the questions. (INTERPRETIVE)

1.

(TRADITIONAL)

　　如果你沒去過城南的"小吃一條街"，你一定得去看看。那兒有很多餐館，湖南的，四川的，上海的，廣東的，都是傳統建築。一到晚上，建築上和馬路上的燈都亮了，五顏六色，非常漂亮。七點鐘左右，街上就擠滿了人，還有不少老外呢。你可別以為他們是來看那些傳統建築的，其實，他們是來嚐嚐餐館裏的傳統小吃的。有的餐館人太多，得等半個多小時才能買到一份小吃。雖然我們這個城市現在有不少美國快餐店，可是來"小吃一條街"的人還是很多。看來不管是"老中"還是"老外"，大家都喜歡中國的傳統小吃。二十年來，這個城市完全變了，只有"小吃一條街"還保留著自己的特色。

(SIMPLIFIED)

　　如果你没去过城南的"小吃一条街"，你一定得去看看。那儿有很多餐馆，湖南的，四川的，上海的，广东的，都是传统建筑。一到晚上，建筑上和马路上的灯都亮了，五颜六色，非常漂亮。七点钟左右，街上就挤满了人，还有不少老外呢。你可别以为他们是来看那些传统建筑的，其实，他们是来尝尝餐馆里的传统小吃的。有的餐馆人太多，得等半个多小时才能买到一份小吃。虽然我们这个城市现在有不少美国快餐店，可是来"小吃一条街"的人还是很多。看来不管是"老中"还是"老外"，大家都喜欢中国的传统小吃。二十年来，这个城市完全变了，只有"小吃一条街"还保留着自己的特色。

Questions (True/False):

( ) **1.** The street described in the passage is in the north part of the city.

( ) **2.** Along the street, there are Chinese restaurants serving different styles of cuisine.

( ) **3.** In the evening, the street is full of people appreciating the architecture.

( ) **4.** According to the passage, it takes over half an hour to reach some of the restaurants.

( ) **5.** In this city, traditional Chinese snacks continue to enjoy popularity in spite of the increasing number of American fast food restaurants.

Questions (Multiple Choice):

( ) **6.** Based on the passage, which of these statements is most accurate?

a. This street is the only place in the city where one can have traditional Chinese food.

b. This street is the only place in the city that has remained largely unchanged over the last two decades.

c. This street is the only place in the city where one cannot find an American fast food restaurant.

( ) **7.** Who do you think is the intended reader of this passage?

a. a restaurant owner

b. an architect

c. a visitor to the city

2.

(TRADITIONAL)

廣生，

看到你昨天的電子郵件，知道你計畫暑假回廣州，我太高興了，真希望暑假明天就開始。我特別高興的是，你沒忘記我們以前常去的"新光"電影院。我和你一樣，也很希望我們能一起再去那兒看一次電影。可是我得告訴你，"新光"電影院那裏半年前蓋了一個新的地鐵站。你知道我們這兒以前是一個很安靜的地方，可是有了地鐵以後，就越來越熱鬧了。還記得"新光"電影院對面的那兩家小鞋店嗎？那兒現在變成了一家日本銀行和一家美國快餐店了。你在法國的這兩年，廣州的變化的確是太大了。不過，對你來說，廣州不會是一個完全陌生的地方，因為我在廣州，我還是兩年前的我。

小花

(SIMPLIFIED)

广生，

看到你昨天的电子邮件，知道你计划暑假回广州，我太高兴了，真希望暑假明天就开始。我特别高兴的是，你没忘记我们以前常去的"新光"电影院。我和你一样，也很希望我们能一起再去那儿看一次电影。可是我得告诉你，"新光"电影院那里半年前盖了一个新的地铁站。你知道我们这儿以前是一个很安静的地方，可是有了地铁以后，就越来越热闹了。还记得"新光"电影院对面的那两家小鞋店吗？那儿现在变成了一家日本银行和一家美国快餐店了。你在法国的这两年，广州的变化的确是太大了。不过，对你来说，广州不会是一个完全陌生的地方，因为我在广州，我还是两年前的我。

小花

Questions (True/False):

(　) **1.** Guangsheng left Guangzhou for France two years ago.

(　) **2.** This email was most likely written in August.

(　) **3.** When Guangsheng was in Guangzhou, he lived close to a subway station.

(　) **4.** When Guangsheng is back in Guangzhou, Xiaohua will see a movie with him at the cinema where they used to go.

Questions (Multiple Choice):

(　) **5.** Which of the following was most likely mentioned in Guangsheng's email to Xiaohua?
　　a. the cinema
　　b. the subway station
　　c. the shoe stores

( ) **6.** What does Xiaohua mean by the final sentence of the message?

　　a. She tries to assure Guangsheng that, even though Guangzhou has changed a lot, he will not get lost in the city.

　　b. She tries to assure Guangsheng that, despite the changes in their part of the city, Guangzhou remains largely the same.

　　c. She tries to assure Guangsheng that she remains the same person and will make Guangsheng feel at home in Guangzhou.

( ) **7.** What is the most likely relationship between the two persons?

　　a. teacher and student

　　b. boyfriend and girlfriend

　　c. casual acquaintances

E. Look at the store sign and answer the questions. (INTERPRETIVE/PRESENTATIONAL)

1. 張天明從來沒去過這個城市，你呢？
　　张天明从来没去过这个城市，你呢？

_____

2. 他們賣的東西裏，你認識哪些？請你選一、兩個翻譯成英文。
　　他们卖的东西里，你认识哪些？请你选一、两个翻译成英文。

_____

F. Look at the slogan and answer the question. (INTERPRETIVE/PRESENTATIONAL)

你已經學過第一句話了，你覺得第二句話的意思是什麼呢？請翻譯成英文。

你已经学过第一句话了，你觉得第二句话的意思是什么呢？请翻译成英文。

IV. Writing and Grammar Exercises

A. Building Characters

Form a character by combining the given components as instructed. Then write a word, a phrase, or a short sentence in which that character appears.

1. 左邊一個"土"，右邊一個"竟然"的"竟"，

   左边一个"土"，右边一个"竟然"的"竟"，

   是 ＿＿＿＿＿＿＿＿＿的＿＿＿＿＿。

2. 外邊一個"銀行"的"行"，中間上、下兩個"土"，

   外边一个"银行"的"行"，中间上、下两个"土"，

   是 ＿＿＿＿＿＿＿＿＿的＿＿＿＿＿。

3. 左邊一個"馬"，右邊一個"奇怪"的"奇"，

   左边一个"马"，右边一个"奇怪"的"奇"，

   是 ＿＿＿＿＿＿＿＿＿的＿＿＿＿＿。

4. 左邊一個"女"，右邊一個"生"，
   左边一个"女"，右边一个"生"，
   是 ＿＿＿＿＿＿＿＿＿的＿＿＿＿＿ 。

5. 外邊一個"广"，裏邊一個"坐"，
   外边一个"广"，里边一个"坐"，
   是 ＿＿＿＿＿＿＿＿＿的＿＿＿＿＿ 。

B. Who knew? Complete the following sentences with 竟(然).

1. 天氣預報説今天天氣會很好，可是下午
   天气预报说今天天气会很好，可是下午

   ＿＿＿＿＿＿＿＿＿＿＿＿＿＿＿＿＿＿ 。

2. 今天是張天明母親的生日，沒想到他
   今天是张天明母亲的生日，没想到他

   ＿＿＿＿＿＿＿＿＿＿＿＿＿＿＿＿＿ 。

3. 張天明以為他能找到父親的中學，但是中學
   张天明以为他能找到父亲的中学，但是中学

   ＿＿＿＿＿＿＿＿＿＿＿＿＿＿＿＿＿＿＿＿ 。

4. 麗莎以為南京是個安靜的小城，沒想到南京
   丽莎以为南京是个安静的小城，没想到南京

   ＿＿＿＿＿＿＿＿＿＿＿＿＿＿＿＿＿＿＿＿ 。

C. Complete the following sentences with 過/过 or 過了/过了.

1. **A:** 咱們一起去吃早飯吧!
      咱们一起去吃早饭吧!
   B: 早飯，我吃＿＿＿＿＿＿＿ 。
      早饭，我吃＿＿＿＿＿＿＿ 。

2. **A:** 你去＿＿＿＿＿＿＿天津嗎?
      你去＿＿＿＿＿＿＿天津吗?
   B: 去＿＿＿＿＿＿＿，我是兩年前去的。
      去＿＿＿＿＿＿＿，我是两年前去的。

3. **A:** 粽子好吃嗎？

　　粽子好吃吗？

　B: 我不知道，我没吃＿＿＿＿＿＿＿＿＿＿。

4. **A:** "民以食為天" 這句話你聽說＿＿＿＿＿＿＿＿＿嗎？

　　"民以食为天" 这句话你听说＿＿＿＿＿＿＿＿＿吗？

　B: 聽說＿＿＿＿＿＿＿＿＿，但不懂什麼意思。

　　听说＿＿＿＿＿＿＿＿＿，但不懂什么意思。

5. **A:** 這本書可以借給我看看嗎？

　　这本书可以借给我看看吗？

　B: 可以，我看＿＿＿＿＿＿＿＿＿，你拿去看吧。

D. Reaffirm A's assumptions by using 的確/的确.

EXAMPLE:

　A: 春節那天北京很熱鬧吧？

　　春节那天北京很热闹吧？

→ **B:** <u>春節那天北京的確很熱鬧</u>。

　　<u>春节那天北京的确很热闹</u>。

1. **A:** 舅媽做的清蒸魚味道不錯吧？

　　舅妈做的清蒸鱼味道不错吧？

→ **B:** ＿＿＿＿＿＿＿＿＿＿＿＿＿＿＿＿＿＿＿＿＿＿＿＿＿＿。

2. **A:** 除夕的春節晚會很有意思吧？

　　除夕的春节晚会很有意思吧？

→ **B:** ＿＿＿＿＿＿＿＿＿＿＿＿＿＿＿＿＿＿＿＿＿＿＿＿＿＿。

3. **A:** 張天明的父親熟悉的南京已經變得完全不一樣了吧？

　　张天明的父亲熟悉的南京已经变得完全不一样了吧？

→ **B:** ＿＿＿＿＿＿＿＿＿＿＿＿＿＿＿＿＿＿＿＿＿＿＿＿＿＿。

4. **A:** 夫子廟是個很有特色的地方吧？

　　夫子庙是个很有特色的地方吧？

→ **B:** ＿＿＿＿＿＿＿＿＿＿＿＿＿＿＿＿＿＿＿＿＿＿＿＿＿＿。

5. A: 張天明是不是覺得中國已經融入國際社會了？

張天明是不是觉得中国已经融入国际社会了？

→ **B:** _____ 。

E. If not for… Complete the sentences with 要不是.

EXAMPLE:

要不是<u>出租汽車師傅幫忙</u>，張天明是不可能找回他的電腦的。
要不是<u>出租汽车师傅帮忙</u>，张天明是不可能找回他的电脑的。

1.

→ _____，柯林上課肯定遲到。

柯林上課肯定遲到。
柯林上课肯定迟到。

2.

→ _____，丽莎还以为她在纽约呢。

麗莎還以為她在紐約呢。
丽莎还以为她在纽约呢。

3.

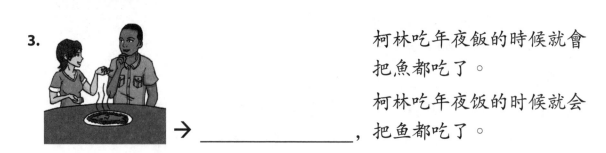

→ _____，把鱼都吃了。

柯林吃年夜飯的時候就會
把魚都吃了。

柯林吃年夜饭的时候就会
把鱼都吃了。

F. Based on the visual clues, complete the following mini-dialogues using 看來/看来.

1. A: 他今天晚上會來嗎？

他今天晚上会来吗？

→ **B:** _____ 。

2. A: 柯林喜歡吃月餅嗎？

柯林喜欢吃月饼吗？

→ **B:** _____ 。

3. A: 雪梅會滑冰嗎？

雪梅会滑冰吗？

→ **B:** _____ 。

4. A: 雪梅舅舅、舅媽兩個人感情怎麼樣？

雪梅舅舅、舅妈两个人感情怎么样？

→ **B:** _____ 。

G. Translate the following dialogues into Chinese. (PRESENTATIONAL)

1. A: Cousin, we've arrived at the train station. Where are you?

B: I'm almost there, too. Sorry, there are many cars on the road. You're not familiar with the city, so don't go running around.

A: Where should we wait for you, then?

B: When you come out of the train station, there's a shopping center next to it. Wait for me at the entrance of the shopping center.

A: OK.

_____

_____

_____

_____

2. A: What's the sound?

B: Sorry, it's my stomach rumbling. I'm hungry.

A: What would you like to eat? There are many snack bars across the street.

B: Do you want to have zongzi?

A: Since it's the Lantern Festival today, let's have Lantern Festival dumplings.

_____

_____

_____

H. Translate the following passage into Chinese. (PRESENTATIONAL)

1. Lisa's Diary

Today Tianming's cousin acted as our tour guide and took us to walk around the streets and see a bit of Nanjing. Tianming's father often says that Nanjing is a quiet city. Who knew it would be this lively and bustling with activity? There are foreign tourists everywhere. There are American fast food restaurants, Japanese banks, and French clothing stores in Nanjing. Tianming said that Nanjing had melded into the world, and that that was a good thing. But I worry that if things go on like this, there could be fewer and fewer things with Chinese characteristics. Tianming's cousin said that Nanjing had preserved many things with Chinese characteristics, for example the Temple of Confucius. After we saw it, we all felt it was really interesting. It seems that people in Nanjing do really want to preserve the traditions of old Nanjing as much as possible.

_____

_____

_____

_____

_____

_____

_____

_____

_____

2. Zhang Tianming's diary

Yesterday we took a high-speed train from Shanghai; it only took two hours to get to Nanjing. The train was very clean and very comfortable, too. My cousin drove to the train station to pick us up. This morning, as soon as we'd had breakfast we went looking for Dad's high school. Who knew? The school was nowhere to be seen, because it had become a big shopping center. The Nanjing that Dad knew so well isn't there any more. Nowadays there are new high-rises everywhere in Nanjing. Streets are crowded with cars. If Dad could see Nanjing's transformation, what would he think?

_____

_____

_____

_____

3. OK. We've arrived at the Temple of Confucius. I'll give a short introduction to the history of the Temple of Confucius. It was first (最早) built in 1034, so Nanjing's Temple of Confucius has a history of almost a thousand years. The architecture that we see now isn't as old as that, but it is very characteristic of Old Nanjing. We can all see that there are many Chinese and foreign tourists here. So who was Confucius? He was a very famous philosopher. In the past, many places in China had a Temple of Confucius. Many people would go to the Temple of Confucius to pay their respects to Confucius (拜孔子), hoping that they would do well on exams.

_____

_____

_____

_____

_____

_____

_____

I. After studying this lesson, write a paragraph in Chinese offering your advice to someone promoting tourism in a city or any other place with a long history. Use at least two grammar patterns and five words and phrases from this lesson. (PRESENTATIONAL)

L. Storytelling (PRESENTATIONAL)

Write a story in Chinese based on the four cartoons below. Make sure that your story has a beginning, a middle, and an end. Also make sure that the transition from one picture to the next is smooth and logical.

1

2

3

4

第十三課　　旅遊

第十三课　　旅游

I. Listening Comprehension

A. Textbook Content (INTERPRETIVE)

Listen to the recording for the Textbook and answer the questions in English.

1. What type of train accommodations did Zhang Tianming choose? Why?

三餐　yíng wò 票 上po, 安靜,干

2. How did Zhang Tianming like the food on the train?

3. How did Zhang Tianming and his friends meet up with their tour guide?

4. How would you describe the scenic spot of Shilin?

5. Among the group, who enjoyed shopping for souvenirs, and who didn't?

6. When Zhang Tianming and his friends spent the evening in Lijiang, what did they do before returning to the hotel?

B. Workbook Dialogue (INTERPRETIVE)

Listen to the recording for the Workbook and answer the questions.

Questions (True/False):

( )　**1.**　The man and woman recently went to Lijiang together.

( )　**2.**　If the woman had wanted to save time, she could have had meals in her hotel.

( )　**3.**　The woman didn't like the souvenir stores in her hotel.

( )　**4.**　The woman didn't look for a family-run bed-and-breakfast, because she thought it would be more expensive.

( ) **5.** According to the man, staying at a bed-and-breakfast would help one get to know the local customs and culture better.

( ) **6.** According to the man, only the big hotels in Lijiang would provide free internet access.

( ) **7.** If this conversation had taken place before the woman's trip, she would have stayed at a different place in Lijiang.

C. Workbook Narratives (INTERPRETIVE)

Listen to the recording for the Workbook and answer the questions in English.

1. Questions:

a. On the speaker's recent trip, what city did he depart from and what city was his destination?

_____

b. What were the two reasons that the speaker chose to buy a soft-berth ticket?

_____

c. Did the speaker have a good night's sleep? Why or why not?

_____

2. Questions:

a. What city did the speaker travel to recently? With whom?

_____

b. What things were covered by the fees they paid to the group tour?

_____

c. Was the speaker completely satisfied with the group tour? Why or why not?

_____

d. What advice does the speaker give?

_____

D. Workbook Listening Rejoinder (INTERPERSONAL)

In this section, you will hear two people talking. After hearing the first speaker, select the best from the four possible responses given by the second speaker.

_____

II. Speaking Exercises

A. Practice asking and answering the following questions. (INTERPERSONAL)

1. 你喜歡參加旅行團還是自己去旅遊？

你喜欢参加旅行团还是自己去旅游？

2. 對你來說，參加旅行團時，什麼最重要？

对你来说，参加旅行团时，什么最重要？

3. 你覺得旅行團的團費應該包括什麼？

你觉得旅行团的团费应该包括什么？

B. Practice speaking on the following topics. (PRESENTATIONAL)

1. 請談談如果你在中國坐火車旅行，你會買硬臥還是買軟臥的車票。為什麼？

请谈谈如果你在中国坐火车旅行，你会买硬卧还是买软卧的车票。为什么？

2. 請談談看了課文後，你想不想去雲南旅遊。為什麼？

请谈谈看了课文后，你想不想去云南旅游。为什么？

3. Describe your ideal vacation trip, including destinations (historic sites, natural scenic sites, etc.), season, means of transportation, joining a tour group or traveling independently, etc.

III. Reading Comprehension

A. Building Words

Complete this section by writing the characters, the *pinyin*, and the English equivalent of each new word formed. Guess the meaning before you use a dictionary to confirm.

1. "分享"的"享" + "受到"的"受"

→ _____ _____ _____

　　　　　　　　　new word　　*pinyin*　　English

2. "硬臥"的"硬" + "軟件"的"件"

"硬卧"的"硬" + "软件"的"件"

→ _____ _____ _____

3. "起床" 的 "床" + "臥鋪" 的 "鋪"

   "起床" 的 "床" + "卧铺" 的 "铺"

   → _____ _____ _____

4. "包括" 的 "包" + "車廂" 的 "廂"

   "包括" 的 "包" + "车厢" 的 "厢"

   → _____ _____ _____

5. "方便麵" 的 "麵" + "一條河" 的 "條"

   "方便面" 的 "面" + "一条河" 的 "条"

   → _____ _____ _____

B. Form a complete sentence by matching each construction on the left with an appropriate phrase on the right.

1. 張天明很馬虎，常常 張天明很马虎，常常	**a.** 五顏六色的 五颜六色的
2. 張天明的房間常常是 張天明的房间常常是	**b.** 一乾二淨的 一干二净的
3. 柯林每頓飯都吃得 柯林每顿饭都吃得	**c.** 千奇百怪的
4. 夫子廟附近很熱鬧，賣的東西 夫子庙附近很热闹，卖的东西	**d.** 丟三拉四的
5. 石林石頭的樣子 石林石头的样子	**e.** 亂七八糟的 乱七八糟的

C. Fill in the blanks with the words provided below:

(TRADITIONAL)

親眼	親自	親耳	親手	親身

1. 沒有去過中國就不能_____感覺到中國節日的氣氛。

2. 這次天明和麗莎_____看到了雲南美麗的風景。

3. 你是_____聽見她說她和她的男朋友吹了嗎？

4. 麗莎很喜歡這件襯衫，因為是她_____做的。

5. 對不起，別人不能幫你申請去中國留學，你得_____申請。

(SIMPLIFIED)

亲眼　　　亲自　　　亲耳　　　亲手　　　亲身

1. 没有去过中国就不能_____感觉到中国节日的气氛。

2. 这次天明和丽莎_____看到了云南美丽的风景。

3. 你是_____听见她说她和她的男朋友吹了吗？

4. 丽莎很喜欢这件衬衫，因为是她_____做的。

5. 对不起，别人不能帮你申请去中国留学，你得_____申请。

D. Read the passages and answer the questions. (INTERPRETIVE)

1.

(TRADITIONAL)

　　我認識大理的一位陳先生，他和太太開家庭旅館。大理附近的旅遊景點很多，一年四季都有不少遊客，不過這幾年因為家庭旅館越來越多，有的家庭旅館常常沒人去住。可是陳先生的家庭旅館幾乎每天都住得滿滿的，沒有空房間。為什麼呢？

　　原來陳先生家的房間雖然不大，可是特別乾淨，而且遊客還可以上網。給遊客做的早飯味道也很好，很有大理的特色。遊客吃完早飯，陳先生就開車送他們去附近的景點。另外，遊客離開的時候，陳先生還送給每人一件紀念品。這樣一來，陳先生陳太太和不少遊客就成了朋友，這些遊客很高興也很願意把他們的家庭旅館介紹給別人，所以來住的遊客就越來越多了。下個月你去大理玩兒，去那兒住兩天，親眼看看，就會看到他們和別的家庭旅館不一樣的地方。

(SIMPLIFIED)

　　我认识大理的一位陈先生，他和太太开家庭旅馆。大理附近的旅游景点很多，一年四季都有不少游客，不过这几年因为家庭旅馆越来越多，有的家庭旅馆常常没人去住。可是陈先生的家庭旅馆几乎每天都住得满满的，没有空房间。为什么呢？

　　原来陈先生家的房间虽然不大，可是特别干净，而且游客还可以上网。给游客做的早饭味道也很好，很有大理的特色。游客吃完早饭，陈先生就开车送他们去附近的景点。另外，游客离开的时候，陈先生还送给每人一件纪念品。这样一来，陈先生陈太太和不少游客就成了朋友，这些游客很高兴也很愿意把他们的家庭旅馆介绍给别人，所以来住的游客就越来越多了。下个月你去大理玩儿，去那儿住两天，亲眼看看，就会看到他们和别的家庭旅馆不一样的地方。

Questions (True/False):

( ) **1.** Mr. and Mrs. Chen own a bed–and–breakfast in Dali.

( ) **2.** Because Dali is a famous tourist destination, business has been booming for all the bed–and–breakfasts there in the recent years.

( ) **3.** Their breakfast accommodates the tourists' different dietary preferences.

( ) **4.** After breakfast, the tourists don't have to worry about transportation to the nearby scenic spots.

Questions (Multiple Choice):

( ) **5.** The good reputation of the Chens' bed–and–breakfast is based on _____.

　　a. good price, internet access, souvenirs as gifts, and transportation to nearby tourist spots

　　b. internet access, transportation to nearby tourist spots, good breakfast, and large rooms

　　c. clean rooms, good breakfast, transportation to nearby tourist spots, and souvenirs as gifts

( ) **6.** Which of the following can be said of the intended reader of this passage?

　　a. He or she is curious about the management of a bed–and–breakfast.

　　b. He or she is planning to travel to Dali as a tourist soon and needs a place to stay.

　　c. He or she is interested in getting to know the reasons for the Chens' success.

2.

(TRADITIONAL)

　　朋友，您生活在熱鬧的大城市上海，每天看到的都是高樓汽車，會不會擔心有中國傳統特色的東西越來越少了呢？想不想親眼去看一個保留了很多傳統建築的古城？離上海不遠的地方就有這樣一個小小的古城，叫周莊 (Zhōuzhuāng)。周莊有九百多年的歷史，很多房子都是一兩百年前蓋的。朋友，從上海來周莊遊覽吧！坐在周莊安靜的茶館裏，一邊喝茶，一邊看外邊的小河和門旁的紅燈籠，您會覺得這是一次最好的旅遊。如果您想報名參加我們的旅遊團，請打1234-5678。團費150元，包括交通，午餐和景點門票。

(SIMPLIFIED)

　　朋友，您生活在热闹的大城市上海，每天看到的都是高楼汽车，会不会担心有中国传统特色的东西越来越少了呢？想不想亲眼去看一个保留了很多传统建筑的古城？离上海不远的地方就有这样一个小小的古城，叫周庄 (Zhōuzhuāng)。周庄有九百多年的历史，很多房子都是一两百年前盖的。朋友，从上海来周庄游览吧！坐在周庄安静的茶馆里，一边喝茶，一边看外边的小河和门旁的红灯笼，您会觉得这是一次最好的旅游。如果您想报名参加我们的旅游团，请打1234-5678。团费150元，包括交通，午餐和景点门票。

Questions (True/False):

( )　**1.**　This is an advertisement that would most likely be seen in Zhouzhuang.

( )　**2.**　People from Shanghai started to visit Zhouzhuang over nine hundred years ago.

( )　**3.**　Many houses in Zhouzhuang are one or two centuries old.

( )　**4.**　The writer implies that there is not much traditional architecture in Shanghai.

( )　**5.**　According to the advertisement, Zhouzhuang's teahouses have the best tea.

Questions (Multiple Choice):

( )　**6.**　In the advertisement, what is presented as the primary selling point of Zhouzhuang?

　　　a. its proximity to Shanghai

　　　b. its contrast to Shanghai

　　　c. its hospitality to tourists from Shanghai

( ) **7.**   What expenses are covered by the 150 yuan paid to the group tour?

   a. round-trip transportation, one meal, and admission tickets

   b. bus ride to Zhouzhuang, lunch and tea, and admission tickets

   c. round-trip bus ride, admission tickets, souvenirs, and lunch

E. Look at the following and answer the questions. (INTERPRETIVE/PRESENTATIONAL)

 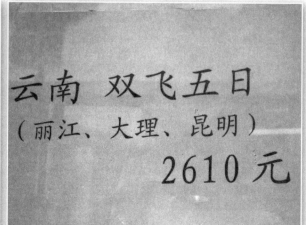

1. 這個廣告是什麼樣的公司貼的？

   这个广告是什么样的公司贴的？

_____

2. 廣告說什麼，請你翻譯成英文。

   广告说什么，请你翻译成英文。

_____

F. Look at the following and answer the question. (INTERPRETIVE/PRESENTATIONAL)

學生考試之前來這個辦公室做什麼?

学生考试之前来这个办公室做什么?

_____

G.

- 豐富三至五星酒店隨心選擇
- 出發日期、停留天數自由決定
- 全國二十餘個出發城市
- 自由行、半自助遊、團隊遊
  不同渡假方式
- 接送機、觀光遊、景點門票等
  可提前預訂
- 獨家推出香港自由行 PASS

- 丰富三至五星酒店随心选择
- 出发日期、停留天数自由决定
- 全国二十余个出发城市
- 自由行、半自助游、团队游
  不同度假方式
- 接送机、观光游、景点门票等
  可提前预订
- 独家推出香港自由行 PASS

This is a travel agency's ad. List in English at least three things that may attract you to sign up for a tour with the agency. (INTERPRETIVE)

_____

IV. Writing and Grammar Exercises

A. Building Characters

Form a character by combining the given components as instructed. Then write a word, a phrase, or a short sentence in which that character appears.

1. 左邊一個"石頭"的"石"，右邊一個"更"，

   左边一个"石头"的"石"，右边一个"更"，

   是 ＿＿＿＿＿＿＿的＿＿＿＿ 。

2. 左邊一個"開車"的"車"，右邊一個"欠錢"的"欠"，

   左边一个"开车"的"车"，右边一个"欠钱"的"欠"，

   是 ＿＿＿＿＿＿＿的＿＿＿＿ 。

3. 左邊一個"口"，右邊一個"在乎"的"乎"，

   左边一个"口"，右边一个"在乎"的"乎"，

   是 ＿＿＿＿＿＿＿的＿＿＿＿ 。

4. 左邊一個提手旁，右邊一個"包"，

   左边一个提手旁，右边一个"包"，

   是 ＿＿＿＿＿＿＿的＿＿＿＿ 。

5. 上邊一個竹字頭，下邊一個"望子成龍"的"龍"，

   上边一个竹字头，下边一个"望子成龙"的"龙"，

   是 ＿＿＿＿＿＿＿的＿＿＿＿ 。

B. Indicate the two separate actions by using 分別.

EXAMPLE:

Little Zhang departed from Guangzhou and Little Li departed from Harbin yesterday.

→ 小張和小李昨天分別從廣州和哈爾濱出發。

小张和小李昨天分别从广州和哈尔滨出发。

1. Teacher Wang's class stayed at a big hotel and Teacher Ke's class stayed at a family-owned bed-and-breakfast.

→ ＿＿＿＿＿＿＿＿＿＿＿＿＿＿＿＿＿＿＿＿＿＿＿

2. Tomorrow my tour group will go to Kunming and her tour group will go to Lijiang.

→ 旅行团 ＿＿＿＿＿＿＿＿＿＿＿＿＿＿＿＿＿＿＿＿

3. Old Tian bought a soft-berth sleeper ticket and Little Tian bought a hard-berth sleeper ticket.

→ _____

4. The older brother slept on the upper bunk and the younger brother slept on the lower bunk.

上 铺
pù

→ _____

5. For lunch, the older sister had a box lunch and the younger sister had noodles.

吃 了

→ _____

C. Rewrite the following sentences as shown in the example.

EXAMPLE:

麗莎對南京夫子廟的印象很深。

丽莎对南京夫子庙的印象很深。

→ <u>南京夫子廟給麗莎留下了很深的印象。</u>

<u>南京夫子庙给丽莎留下了很深的印象。</u>

1. 雪梅的舅舅對柯林的印象很好。

雪梅的舅舅对柯林的印象很好。

→ _____

2. 天明對那家紀念品商店的印象不太好。

天明对那家纪念品商店的印象不太好。

→ _____

3. 天明對南京城市的變化印象很深。

天明对南京城市的变化印象很深。

→ _____

4. 雪梅對舅舅住的小區印象很不錯。

雪梅对舅舅住的小区印象很不错。

→ _____

D. Based on the texts in the lessons and the clues below, compare A and B and describe how they differ using the three different structures as shown.

EXAMPLE: A: joining a tour   B: traveling on his own

→ 張天明覺得參加旅行團沒有自助遊自由。
　張天明觉得参加旅行团没有自助游自由。

→ 張天明覺得參加旅行團不如自助遊自由。
　張天明觉得参加旅行团不如自助游自由。

→ 張天明覺得自助遊比參加旅行團自由。
　張天明觉得自助游比参加旅行团自由。

1.   A: chatting online   B: chatting on the phone

→ _____

→ _____

→ _____

2.   A: having a happy childhood   B: being successful as an adult

→ _____

→ _____

→ _____

3.   A: spending the New Year in the US   B: spending the Chinese New Year in China

→ _____

→ _____

→ _____

E. Based on the lessons and the information given, complete the following statements by using 只好.

1. 舅舅舅媽本來打算在餐館訂餐吃年夜飯，但家家都沒位子，
   舅舅舅妈本来打算在餐馆订餐吃年夜饭，但家家都没位子，

   _____ 。

2. 柯林、天明覺得旅遊時買紀念品很浪費時間，可是他們參加的是
   有購物的團，所以
   柯林、天明觉得旅游时买纪念品很浪费时间，可是他们参加的是
   有购物的团，所以

   _____ 。

3. 天明、麗莎還想繼續在南京街上邊走邊拍照，但表哥肚子餓了，
   天明、丽莎还想继续在南京街上边走边拍照，但表哥肚子饿了，

   _____ 。

F. Based on the visual clues, give your advice or warning by using 千萬/千万.

EXAMPLE: 生病

→ <u>生病的時候，千萬別亂吃藥</u>。
  <u>生病的时候，千万别乱吃药</u>。

1. 睡覺/睡觉

→ _____

2. 出門/出门

→ _____

3. 下出租車/下出租车

→ _____

4. 過春節/过春节

→ _____

G. Complete the sentences with 不過/不过 (no more than). (INTERPRETIVE/PRESENTATIONAL)

1.

這家商店的衣服很便宜，一條牛仔褲
这家商店的衣服很便宜，一条牛仔裤

_____ ○

2.

還早，你再坐一會兒吧。現在
还早，你再坐一会儿吧。现在

_____ ○

3.

這棟樓不高，
这栋楼不高，

_____ ○

4.

他的老家不大，人口

_____ ○

H. Translate the following dialogues into Chinese. (PRESENTATIONAL)

1. A: Do you need a box lunch?

　　B: Do you have vegetarian box lunches?

　　A: Sorry, vegetarian box lunches are sold out.

　　B: What else do you have?

　　A: We also have instant noodles.

　　B: Then I'll buy instant noodles.

你要一个盒饭吗？你有素的盒饭吗？对不其，素的卖光了。
你还有什么？我也有方便面。我买方便面吧。

2. A: Dad, would you like to take (sleep in) the upper bunk or lower bunk? The upper bunk is quieter; you can have a good night's sleep. The lower bunk is more convenient.

　　B: Then I'll take the lower bunk. I brought an extra blanket and pillow from home. Do you need them?

　　A: One blanket and one pillow are enough for me. You like to use two pillows—why don't you use the pillow from home?

爸爸，你想睡在上铺还是下铺？上铺比较安静，你
能睡好觉。下铺比较方便。我睡在下铺吧。我带了毯子
和枕头，你要吗？一个毯子和枕头够了。你喜欢用两个
枕头，你用吧？

3. A: Hi, Mom. We've returned to Beijing from Yunnan.

　　B: Is that so? How did you get to Yunnan?

　　A: We signed up online and joined a tour group. Then we took a train to Kunming and waited for Xuemei and Ke Lin.

　　B: What kind of train did you take?

　　A: We wanted to practice speaking Chinese with the other passengers, so Lisa and I bought two tickets for a hard sleeper.

　　B: Which places did you go?

　　A: We went to Shilin, Dali, and Lijiang. We also went to see the big snow mountain.

　　B: What was your impression of Yunnan?

A: Yunnan was really interesting! The landscape of each place was different. There were many fun places we didn't have time to go to.

B: Next time, then.

妈,我们从云南回到了北京了。是吗?你怎么去了云南?

我们在网上报名参加了旅行团。我们火车坐到昆明,等雪

梅和可林。你们坐了什么样的火车?因为我们想练习

说中文所以买了两张硬卧票。你们去了哪儿?去了石林、

大理和丽江,也看了大雪山。你对云南的印象怎么样?

云南很有意思。每个地方的风景不样,有很多好玩的地

方没时间去。下一次吧。

呢

I. Translate the following passages into Chinese. (PRESENTATIONAL)

1. Tianming's email to Lisa:

Lisa:

I checked online. There are many places in Yunnan with beautiful scenery. We can do a self-guided tour:

The first day—Shilin, staying at a 3-star (三星级/三星级) hotel

The second day—Dali, visiting the Three Pagodas of Dali, staying at a 4-star (四星级/四星级) hotel

The third day—Lijiang's Old City, staying at a family-run hotel

How do you feel about this? We'll take a train to Kunming first. Ke Lin and Xuemei would also like to go to Yunnan. We can meet up in Kunming.

Tianming

丽莎:

我网上查了。云南很多地方的风景很漂亮。我们可以自己做

导游。第一天一石林,住在三星级的旅馆。第二天一大理,看大

理三塔,住在四星级的旅馆。第三天-丽江的老城市,住在家庭

旅馆。这么样?我们先坐火车去昆明。可林和雪梅也想

去云南,可以在昆明见面。天明

更自由 ✓
自由多 ✗

2. Lisa's reply to Tianming

Tianming:

I'd like to travel on our own, because we'd have more freedom. However, we just got to China—I think it'd be more convenient for us to join a tour group. This way we wouldn't have to book hotels, or buy admission tickets. If we went to a different place every day to travel on our own, it'd be very exhausting (we'd be very tired). A tour group would have a tour guide to introduce us to Yunnan's architecture, clothes, and food and help us learn about each ethnic group's customs. What do you say?

Lisa

天明：我想我们俩旅行，自由多~更~。我们 刚刚到了中国，参加一个旅行团更方便 吧？这样不要约旅馆或者买门票。如果自己每天去另外的地方，就太累了。旅行团有导游介绍云南的建筑，服装，食物，也教我们民族的风俗。怎么样？

丽莎。   习惯

3. Last year we went to England and stayed at a family hotel. Behind the hotel, there was a small river. The hotel wasn't very big, and it was very quiet and very clean, too. The owner cooked family-style dishes for us. They tasted very nice. The owner said that the fish that he made for us came from the river behind the hotel, so it was very fresh.

去年我去了英国，住在一家家庭旅馆。旅馆后面有一条小河。旅馆不太大，又安静又干净。房东给我们做了些家常菜，味道很好。房东说他做了一条鱼是从小河拿所以很香。

新鲜 - fresh

J. Propose a three-, five-, or seven-day tour itinerary for tourists visiting your hometown or your favorite place. Make sure to include means of transportation, places to stay, scenic spots to visit, tour guide's specialties, fees that will be charged, etc. Title your itinerary 《[Name of the place] 三(五、七) 日遊／游 》(PRESENTATIONAL)

K. Storytelling (PRESENTATIONAL)

Write a story in Chinese based on the four cartoons below. Make sure that your story has a beginning, a middle, and an end. Also make sure that the transition from one picture to the next is smooth and logical.

1

2

3

4

14 第十四課   生活與健康
第十四课   生活与健康

I. Listening Comprehension

A. Textbook Content (INTERPRETIVE)

Listen to the recording for the Textbook and answer the questions in English.

1. Does Lisa have to pay monthly rent to her landlord? Why or why not?

她不必付家租因为她教房东的女儿中文。

2. What does Lisa see every morning when she takes a walk in the neighborhood?

她看到很多人,很多老人锻炼身体。

3. Why is Lisa getting up so early today, even though it's Saturday?

她本来想跟房去学太极拳,可是他们已经走了。

4. What does Lisa think about gaining or losing weight?

身体健康最重要,胖瘦不重要。

5. According to Lisa and Li Wen, how much should one eat at each meal in order to stay healthy?

早餐要吃好,午餐要吃饱,晚餐要吃少。

6. What health advice does Li Wen find most difficult to follow? Why?

吃三顿菜对她来说最难因为生活很忙。

B. Workbook Dialogue (INTERPRETIVE)

Listen to the recording for the Workbook and answer the questions.

Questions (True/False):

(F) **1.** The daughter has been having small suppers for a long time.

(F) **2.** The father categorically disagrees with the saying that favors small suppers.

(F) **3.** The daughter is scheduled to start working at 7 p.m. tonight.

(F) **4.** The father has never worked on a night shift before.

(T) **5.** Despite the father's admonition, the daughter won't eat more for dinner.

(T) **6.** According to the daughter, the quantity of food does not mean the same thing as nutrition.

C. Workbook Narratives (INTERPRETIVE)

Listen to the recording for the Workbook and answer the questions in English.

1. Questions:

a. Where do Li Wen's parents usually do tai chi in the early morning?

_____

b. Where did they do tai chi the last couple of days? Why?

_____

c. What did Li Wen do last night?

_____

d. Did Li Wen's parents have their tai chi session this morning as usual? Why or why not?

_____

2. Questions:

a. Are there many Chinese young people practicing tai chi? Why or why not?

_____

b. According to the speaker, do Chinese young people pay much attention to physical health?

_____

c. According to the speaker, what are the most popular forms of physical exercise for young people in China?

_____

D. Workbook Listening Rejoinder (INTERPERSONAL)

In this section, you will hear two people talking. After hearing the first speaker, select the best from the four possible responses given by the second speaker.

_____

II. Speaking Exercises

A. Practice asking and answering the following questions. (INTERPERSONAL)

1. 你做過瑜伽，打過太極拳嗎？

你做过瑜伽，打过太极拳吗？

2. 你覺得瑜伽與太極拳，哪一個的動作更美？

你觉得瑜伽与太极拳，哪一个的动作更美？

3. 你平常怎麼注意身體健康？

你平常怎么注意身体健康？

4. 你有什麼不良的飲食或生活習慣？

你有什么不良的饮食或生活习惯？

B. Practice speaking on the following topics. (PRESENTATIONAL)

1. 請談談你平常怎麼鍛煉身體，包括多久鍛煉一次，每次鍛煉多長時間。

请谈谈你平常怎么锻炼身体，包括多久锻炼一次，每次锻炼多长时间。

2. 請談談你平常做得到做不到"早餐要吃好，午餐要吃飽，晚餐要吃少"。為什麼？

请谈谈你平常做得到做不到"早餐要吃好，午餐要吃饱，晚餐要吃少"。为什么？

3. Describe an ideal lifestyle that you would like to adopt for health and wellness.

III. Reading Comprehension

A. Building Words

Complete this section by writing the characters, the *pinyin*, and the English equivalent of each new word formed. Guess the meaning before you use a dictionary to confirm.

1. "散步" 的 "散" + "心情" 的 "心"

→ _____ _____ _____

　　　　　　new word　　*pinyin*　　English

2. "團圓" 的 "圓" + "站成圈" 的 "圈"

"团圆" 的 "圆" + "站成圈" 的 "圈"

→ _____ _____ _____

3. "排隊" 的 "隊" + "落伍" 的 "伍"

"排队" 的 "队" + "落伍" 的 "伍"

→ _____ _____ _____

4. "打呼嚕" 的 "呼" + "吸煙" 的 "吸"

"打呼噜" 的 "呼" + "吸烟" 的 "吸"

→ _____ _____ _____

5. "補充" 的 "補" + "學習" 的 "習"

"补充" 的 "补" + "学习" 的 "习"

→ _____ _____ _____

B. Read the passages and answer the questions. (INTERPRETIVE)

1.

(TRADITIONAL)

　　老張，好久沒收到你的電子郵件了，最近好嗎？聽說你正在計畫開餐館，肯定很忙。

　　很多人以為開餐館一定會賺錢，其實這要看餐館開在哪兒。你的餐館開在什麼地方最好呢？我說說我的看法，給你一點兒建議。

　　如果你們那兒有一家受歡迎的健身房，你就把餐館開在健身房旁邊，這樣一定會賺錢，這是我的經驗，也是有道理的。為什麼很多人不常去餐館吃飯？不是因為他們沒錢，而是因為他們怕吃多了會越來越胖，對身體沒有好處。可是如果你的餐館旁邊就是健身房，他們吃完飯就去鍛煉，或者鍛煉以後來吃飯，就不會那麼擔心了。怎麼樣？我說的有道理吧？明年你的餐館賺了錢，可別忘了免費請我吃幾頓啊。

(SIMPLIFIED)

　　老张，好久没收到你的电子邮件了，最近好吗？听说你正在计划开餐馆，肯定很忙。

　　很多人以为开餐馆一定会赚钱，其实这要看餐馆开在哪儿。你的餐馆开在什么地方最好呢？我说说我的看法，给你一点儿建议。

　　如果你们那儿有一家受欢迎的健身房，你就把餐馆开在健身房旁边，这样一定会赚钱，这是我的经验，也是有道理的。为什么很多人不常去餐馆吃饭？不是因为他们没钱，而是因为他们怕吃多了会越来越胖，对身体没有好处。可是如果你的餐馆旁边就是健身房，他们吃完饭就去锻炼，或者锻炼以后来吃饭，就不会那么担心了。怎么样？我说的有道理吧？明年你的餐馆赚了钱，可别忘了免费请我吃几顿啊。

Questions (True/False):

( )　**1.**　The writer and Lao Zhang have been exchanging emails frequently.

( )　**2.**　Lao Zhang has owned a restaurant for many years.

( )　**3.**　According to the writer, running a restaurant does not necessarily make money.

( )　**4.**　The writer is looking for a good gym to exercise in.

Questions (Multiple Choice):

( )　**5.**　According to the writer, which is most important to the success of a restaurant?

　　a. its location

　　b. the quality of its food

　　c. the quality of its service

( )　**6.**　The writer believes that the customers will not worry too much about the health effects of restaurant food if _____.

　　a. they don't eat too much every time they visit a restaurant

　　b. they don't eat at restaurants too frequently

　　c. they can exercise at a gym right before or after eating at a restaurant

2.

(TRADITIONAL)

　　毛明今年春天高中畢業，秋天就要上大學了。他學習很好，可是不喜歡運動，所以爸爸媽媽有點兒為他的健康擔心。毛明的生日在七月。過生日那天，爸爸給他的禮物是一套運動服，媽媽送給他一張碟，上面有"姚明 (Yao Ming) 打籃球"幾個字。毛明看了那張碟以後，開始對籃球有點兒興趣了。九月初，毛明去上大學了。十月三十號是爸爸媽媽結婚二十年的紀念日。那天，他們收到了毛明給他們的禮物。他們打開一看，原來也是一張碟，上面有"毛明打籃球"幾個字。爸爸媽媽高興極了。他們看了那張碟以後，再也不為兒子的健康擔心了。

(SIMPLIFIED)

　　毛明今年春天高中毕业，秋天就要上大学了。他学习很好，可是不喜欢运动，所以爸爸妈妈有点儿为他的健康担心。毛明的生日在七月。过生日那天，爸爸给他的礼物是一套运动服，妈妈送给他一张碟，上面有"姚明 (Yao Ming) 打篮球"几个字。毛明看了那张碟以后，开始对篮球有点儿兴趣了。九月初，毛明去上大学了。十月三十号是爸爸妈妈结婚二十年的纪念日。那天，他们收到了毛明给他们的礼物。他们打开一看，原来也是一张碟，上面有"毛明打篮球"几个字。爸爸妈妈高兴极了。他们看了那张碟以后，再也不为儿子的健康担心了。

Questions (True/False):

( ) **1.** Mao Ming's parents were concerned that Mao Ming would not be able to go to a good university.

( ) **2.** When Mao Ming had his eighteenth birthday, his parents sent their birthday gifts to his school.

( ) **3.** Mao Ming's parents have become more confident about their son's health.

Questions (Multiple Choice):

( ) **4.** What was the rationale behind the parents' choice of birthday presents?

  a. They were selected based on Mao Ming's interest.

  b. They were intended to help generate Mao Ming's interest in sports.

  c. They were chosen because of the parents' love for sports.

( ) **5.** What is most likely on the DVD that Mao Ming sent his parents as a gift?

  a. Yao Ming's NBA games

  b. Mao Ming playing basketball in his childhood

  c. Mao Ming playing basketball at his university

C. Look at the following ad sign and answer the questions. (INTERPRETIVE/PRESENTATIONAL)

1. 這個早餐店的名字是希望你在這兒吃早餐以後會覺得怎麼樣？
   这个早餐店的名字是希望你在这儿吃早餐以后会觉得怎么样？

_____

2. 如果在這家店吃早飯，你會點什麼？
   如果在这家店吃早饭，你会点什么？

_____

D. Look at the following notice and answer the questions. (INTERPRETIVE/PRESENTATIONAL)

暑期留學生武術課開課通知

一、　報名選課時間及地點：　6 月 25 日至 7 月 20 日
（中午 1：00~2：00 或 下午 3：30~5：30）前到足球場小
房報名。**報名電話：**

二、上課內容、時間及地點：
　1、太極拳：
　　　早上 6：20—7：10 或 下午 4：00—4：50 每週一至週五上課。
　　　6 月 29 日早上 6：20 在足球場上課。
　2、長拳、劍術：
　　　下午 1：30—2：20 或 下午 4：00—4：50 每週一至週五。
　　　6 月 29 日下午 1：30 在足球場上課。
　注：6 月 29 日以後來的外國同學可插班上課，隨堂報名。　體育教學部
　　　　　　　　　　　　　　　　　　　　　　　　　　　　2009-6-25

暑期留学生武术课开课通知

一、　报名选课时间及地点：　6 月 25 日至 7 月 20 日
（中午 1：00~2：00 或 下午 3：30~5：30）前到足球场小
房报名。报名电话：

二、上课内容、时间及地点：
　1、太极拳：
　　　早上 6：20—7：10 或 下午 4：00—4：50 每周一至周五上课。
　　　6 月 29 日早上 6：20 在足球场上课。
　2、长拳、剑术：
　　　下午 1：30—2：20 或 下午 4：00—4：50 每周一至周五。
　　　6 月 29 日下午 1：30 在足球场上课。
　注：6 月 29 日以后来的外国同学可插班上课，随堂报名。　体育教学部
　　　　　　　　　　　　　　　　　　　　　　　　　　　　2009-6-25

1. 太極拳有幾個班？

太极拳有几个班？　_____

2. 每次上課上多長時間？

每次上课上多长时间？　_____

3. 哪一天開始上課？

哪一天开始上课？　_____

4. 在什麼地方上課？

在什么地方上课？ _____

5. 誰可以報名參加這個太極拳班？

谁可以报名参加这个太极拳班？ _____

6. 報名時間是從什麼時候到什麼時候？

报名时间是从什么时候到什么时候？ _____

IV. Writing and Grammar Exercises

A. Building Characters

Form a character by combining the given components as instructed. Then write a word, a phrase, or a short sentence in which that character appears.

1. 左邊一個金字旁，右邊一個"一段時間"的"段"，

左边一个金字旁，右边一个"一段时间"的"段"，

是 _____的_____ 。

2. 左邊一個提手旁，右邊一個"非常"的"非"，

左边一个提手旁，右边一个"非常"的"非"，

是 _____的_____ 。

3. 左邊一個人字旁，右邊一個"加州"的"加"，

左边一个人字旁，右边一个"加州"的"加"，

是 _____的_____ 。

4. 左邊一個食字旁，右邊一個"包"，

左边一个食字旁，右边一个"包"，

是 _____的_____ 。

5. 左邊一個"口"，右邊一個"來不及"的"及"，

左边一个"口"，右边一个"来不及"的"及"，

是 _____的_____ 。

6. 左邊一個"目"，右邊一個"民以食為天"的"民"，

左边一个"目"，右边一个"民以食为天"的"民"，

是 _____的_____ 。

7. 上邊一個"不"，下邊一個"口"，

上边一个"不"，下边一个"口"，

是 _____的_____ 。

B. Based on the texts in the lessons, answer the following questions. (INTERPRETIVE AND PRESENTATIONAL)

1. 麗莎覺得什麼使北京看起來很有活力？

丽莎觉得什么使北京看起来很有活力？

→ _____

2. 什麼使天明對雲南的印象非常好？

什么使天明对云南的印象非常好？

→ _____

3. 天明擔心什麼事會使父親難過？

天明担心什么事会使父亲难过？

→ _____

4. 麗莎認為什麼能使人身體健康？

丽莎认为什么能使人身体健康？

→ _____

C. In the scenarios below, give encouragement using 只要…就.

EXAMPLE:

A: 我打太極拳，動作不太美。

我打太极拳，动作不太美。

→ **B:** <u>只要多打，動作就會好看</u>

<u>只要多打，动作就会好看</u>

1. A: 我的身體不太好。

我的身体不太好。

→ **B:** 只要注意饮食，就身休会好。

2. A: 我做瑜伽的時候，動作常常會忘。

我做瑜伽的时候，动作常常会忘。

→ **B:** _____

3. A: 我請了英文家教，可是英文還是不進步。

我请了英文家教，可是英文还是不进步。

→ **B:** _____

D. Suppose you are very easygoing. People can do whatever they want, and it's all fine with you. What would you say, using 隨便/随便? (PRESENTATIONAL)

EXAMPLE:

 別客氣，桌子上的水果你隨便吃。
別客气，桌子上的水果你随便吃。

1.

 _____

2.

 _____

Suppose your friend is not so easygoing. What would he or she say, using 隨便/随便?

EXAMPLE:

→ 我的車請你別隨便開。
我的车请你别随便开。

3.

 _____

4.

 _____

E. Based on the information given, use 即使…也… to express your determination to do something despite potential risks or disadvantages.

　　EXAMPLE:

　　A: 我不准你住校外，因為不太安全。

　　　　我不准你住校外，因为不太安全。

→ **B:** 即使不太安全，我也要住校外。

　1.A: 冬天哈爾濱很冷，最好別去。

　　　　冬天哈尔滨很冷，最好别去。

→ **B:** _____ 。

　2.A: 坐船遊覽長江，很花時間，還是算了吧。

　　　　坐船游览长江，很花时间，还是算了吧。

→ **B:** _____ 。

　3.A: 春節夫子廟那兒人山人海，太擠了。我們在家玩遊戲，怎麼樣？

　　　　春节夫子庙那儿人山人海，太挤了。我们在家玩游戏，怎么样？

→ **B:** _____ 。

　4.A: 這套運動服得花你一個月的工資，你非買不可嗎？

　　　　这套运动服得花你一个月的工资，你非买不可吗？

→ **B:** _____ 。

　5.A: 聽說這門金融課實在難學，我決定不選了，你還想選嗎？

　　　　听说这门金融课实在难学，我决定不选了，你还想选吗？

→ **B:** _____ 。

F. Based on the texts in the lessons, describe the given scenario in Chinese, and make an inference from that description by using 可見/可见.

　　EXAMPLE: Li Wen's parents practice tai chi every morning.

→ 李文的父母每天早上都打太極拳，可見他們非常重視鍛煉身體。

　李文的父母每天早上都打太极拳，可见他们非常重视锻炼身体。

　1. Lisa eats a lot of fruit and vegetables.

→ _____

2. Li Wen's eyes look like a panda's eyes.

→ _____

3. Tianming's tour guide made them laugh all the time.

→ _____

4. Xuemei's aunt was busy preparing the New Year's Eve dinner, and her uncle was by her side helping.

→ _____

G. Based on the texts in the lessons and the illustrations below, have the characters of the textbook give their advice or warning using 否則/否则.

EXAMPLE: Tianming's being late

→   麗莎告訴天明千萬別遲到，否則她會跟他吹了。
    丽莎告诉天明千万别迟到，否则她会跟他吹了。

1.   Li Wen's staying up late

→ _____

2.   Lisa's purchasing a soft berth ticket

→ _____

3.   his friend's joining a "shopping" tour

→ _____

H. Translate the following dialogues into Chinese. (PRESENTATIONAL)

1. **A:** Old Li, you should pay more attention to your health, and exercise more.

   B: Doctor, my house is too far away from the gym. It's too inconvenient to go to the gym.

   A: As long as you exercise, it doesn't matter where. You don't need to go to the gym. For example, you can do yoga at home.

   B: I'm an old man. It's a bit weird for me to do yoga.

   A: Old Li, your thinking is problematic. OK, if you don't feel like doing yoga, you can go downstairs and practice tai chi.

   B: Tai chi's movements are too slow. Besides I won't be able to learn it.

   A: Then how about jogging? You won't have to learn (how to jog).

   B: The streets are crowded with cars. It's unsafe. Our residential district is too small. There's no place to jog.

   A: Taking a walk is also great exercise.

   B: I'll consider walking.

老李，你应该注意身体健康，多锻炼身体。

医生，我家离健身房太远，太不方便。

只要锻炼身体就好，不管在那儿，不要去健身房。

比方说，可以在家做瑜伽。

我是老人，做瑜伽很奇怪。

老李，你的想法有问题。好吧，你不想做瑜伽，可以楼下学习太极拳。

太极拳的动作太慢了，再说太极拳我学不起来。

跑步呢？你不必要学。

街上挤满的太危险。小区也太小，没地方跑步。

散步也是很好的运动。

我考虑散步。

2. A: Old Li, I see that you're much healthier.

B: Doctor, I listened to you (your advice/words). Every morning I take a walk.

A: I see that you're not as overweight as before.

B: I used to like eating meat a lot and would seldom eat green leafy vegetables and fruit. I never had breakfasts, ate anything I could for lunch, and had a very large dinner. Now besides taking a walk every day, I've also begun to pay attention to my diet.

A: That's great. Now you have an excellent lifestyle. That's good for your health.

老李,你看起来比以前健康了。

医生,我听着你的建议,每天早上散步。

我看见你减肥了。

我以前喜欢吃多肉,少吃绿叶蔬菜和水果,不吃早饭,

中饭什么都吃,晚饭吃得很多,除了每天散步以外,我

也开始注意了饮食。

真好的,你有很特别的生活,对你的健康有好处。

3. A: Have you seen many older Chinese people exercising in the morning on street corners and in parks?

B: No. After I came to China, I've been staying up late. Look at my panda eyes.

A: I like to go to bed early and get up early. I go out and take a walk after breakfast.

B: I should be like you and have a good lifestyle. I have seen older people dancing on street corners in the evening. It's really interesting.

A: You're right. In my country, generally speaking, everyone pays to go to a gym to exercise by themselves. It's both expensive and boring.

B: I agree. It's the same in my country. Older Chinese people exercising on street corners with friends—how great that is! It doesn't take any money and you can meet with old friends!

你看见了很多老人在街边和公园锻炼身体吗?

没有,到中国以后我每天熬夜,看我的熊猫眼睛。

我喜欢早睡早起,吃早饭以后出去散步。

我应该跟你一样生活好,我晚上看见了老人在街边跳舞,

很有趣。

说的对,在我的国家大家都付钱在健身房自锻炼,

又贵又无聊。

我同意,我的国家一样,老的中国人在街边跟朋友锻炼

身体这么好。不必付钱,也可以跟好朋友见面。

I. Translate the following passages into Chinese. (PRESENTATIONAL)

1. Lin Xuemei's uncle and aunt place a lot of importance on exercise. Although they are almost fifty, they have very good figures, and seem to be full of energy. Ke Lin saw Lin Xuemei's uncle going to the little park in the housing complex every morning to do tai chi and asked Uncle to teach him.

Uncle told Ke Lin that he had been doing tai chi for ten years. As for Aunt, she liked to do yoga in the evenings. Lin Xuemei did yoga with Aunt together. Ke Lin and Lin Xuemei both said that not only did they eat well at Uncle's house, they also learned to pay attention to their health.

林雪梅的舅舅舅妈很重视锻炼身体。虽然他们快五十岁，身材很好，很有活力。柯林看见了雪梅的舅舅每天早晨去小区的小公园去打太极拳，问了舅舅能不能教他。

舅舅告诉了柯林他打太极拳打了十年了。至于舅妈，她喜欢晚上做瑜伽，林雪梅以前是舅妈做。柯林和雪梅俩说除了吃得如以外，在舅舅的家也学了怎么注意健康。

2. Doctor, this is my dog Feifei (肥肥). You see it's very fat. It eats a lot every day and doesn't like to drink water. Its eating habits are very bad, and it's lazy and doesn't like to exercise (運動/运动), so it has many health problems. My sister says this is because my lifestyle is not very good, either. She says I don't have any energy at all, and I should exercise more and pay attention to my diet. She asks me to take Feifei jogging every day. Some people say that dogs will resemble their owners (主人), but my sister says I have to pay attention, otherwise I'll resemble Feifei more and more.

医生，这是我的狗肥肥。可见它很胖。它每吃很多，不喝水吃的习惯很差，很懒，不喜欢运动，健康的问题很多。姐姐说是因为我的生活也不好。她说我没有活力，我应该多运动，注意饮食。她情我每天带肥肥去跑步。有射人说狗会跟主人很像，可是姐姐说我要注意，否则会跟肥肥像。

J. Compare your views on diet, lifestyle, and fitness with Lisa's. Comment on whether you would like to make any changes to improve your lifestyle, or whether you have any advice for Lisa. (PRESENTATIONAL)

K. Storytelling (PRESENTATIONAL)

Write a story in Chinese based on the four cartoons below. Make sure that your story has a beginning, a middle, and an end. Also make sure that the transition from one picture to the next is smooth and logical.

1

2

3

4

15   第十五课   男女平等
第十五课   男女平等

 # I. Listening Comprehension

A. Textbook Content (INTERPRETIVE)

Listen to the recording for the Textbook and answer the questions in English.

1. What was the status of women in traditional Chinese society?

妇女的地位比男人低得多。

2. Can you describe the changes in Chinese women's social and familial status since the 1950s?

男和女受教育和参加工作的机会一样, 社会地位也提高了。

3. What interests and hobbies does Xuemei's uncle have? How do they affect his relationship with his wife?

他是个大球迷。看足球赛就不做家务。

4. How do Xuemei's uncle and aunt split up the household chores?

他们俩一起帮一起

5. Is Xuemei's aunt a fan of the Chinese men's soccer team? Why or why not?

她不是因为足队员老输球。

6. How would you recap the ball game that Xuemei's uncle describes?

男足队比赛结束以前就赢了。

B. Workbook Dialogue (INTERPRETIVE)

Listen to the recording for the Workbook and answer the questions.

Questions (True/False):

(F) **1.** Professor Qian and her husband have lived in the same neighborhood as the speakers since last year.

(T) **2.** The female speaker went to graduate school.

(F) **3.** The male speaker assumes that distinguished professors are usually above forty.

(F) **4.** Professor Qian does all kinds of household chores except for dishwashing.

(T) **5.** The man thinks both Professor Qian and her husband are happy in their marriage.

C. Workbook Narratives (INTERPRETIVE)

Listen to the recording for the Workbook and answer the questions in English.

1. Questions:

a. How would you describe the speaker's attitude toward the men's soccer team?

_____

b. Do you think the woman will watch the soccer game on TV this evening? Why or why not?

_____

c. What does the speaker suggest that the members of the men's soccer team should do?

_____

2. Questions:

a. What are Li Xiaoyang's relationships with the speaker and the speaker's sister?

_____

b. How would you describe the purpose of this message?

_____

c. What is the speaker's impression of Li Xiaoyang, and how did he receive that impression?

_____

d. Has the speaker often met Li Xiaoyang recently? How do you know?

_____

D. Workbook Listening Rejoinder (INTERPERSONAL)

In this section, you will hear two people talking. After hearing the first speaker, select the best from the four possible responses given by the second speaker.

_____

II. Speaking Exercises

A. Practice asking and answering the following questions. (INTERPERSONAL)

1. 你平常在家做什麼家務？

你平常在家做什么家务？

2. 在你的國家，婦女的家庭地位與社會地位跟男人一樣高嗎？

在你的国家，妇女的家庭地位与社会地位跟男人一样高吗？

B. Practice speaking on the following topics. (PRESENTATIONAL)

1. 請談談對你來説什麼樣的夫妻是"模範夫妻"。

請談談对你来说什么样的夫妻是"模范夫妻"。

2. 請你談談社會上有哪些男女不平等的現象。

请你谈谈社会上有哪些男女不平等的现象。

3. Talk about what individuals and society can do about gender inequality.

III. Reading Comprehension

A. Building Words

Complete this section by writing the characters, the *pinyin*, and the English equivalent of each new word formed. Guess the meaning before you use a dictionary to confirm.

1. "困難" 的 "困" + "環境" 的 "境"

"困难" 的 "困" + "环境" 的 "境"

→ _____ _____ _____

　　　　　　　　new word　　*pinyin*　　　English

2. "工廠" 的 "廠" + "房子" 的 "房"

"工厂" 的 "厂" + "房子" 的 "房"

→ _____ _____ _____

3. "事情" 的 "事" + "家務" 的 "務"

"事情" 的 "事" + "家务" 的 "务"

→ _____ _____ _____

4. "討厭" 的 "厭" + "飲食" 的 "食"

"讨厌" 的 "厌" + "饮食" 的 "食"

→ _____ _____ _____

5. "驕傲" 的 "傲" + "快慢" 的 "慢"

"骄傲" 的 "傲" + "快慢" 的 "慢"

→ _____ _____ _____

B. Match the nouns or noun phrases on the left with adjectives on the right to form descriptions of the Chinese men's soccer team.

1.社會地位/社会地位	**a.**驕傲/骄傲
2.球迷	**b.**糟糕
3.比賽成績/比赛成绩	**c.**高
4.態度/态度	**d.**多

C. Read the passages and answer the questions. (INTERPRETIVE)

1.

(TRADITIONAL)

　　蘭蘭今年夏天大學畢業了。她有個哥哥，比她大兩歲，高中畢業後沒考上大學，就去開出租車了。蘭蘭的學習成績比哥哥好，高中畢業後考進了一所名牌大學。她的父母薪水都不高，所以哥哥掙的錢差不多都給蘭蘭付學費了。好不容易等到蘭蘭大學畢業了，大家都以為她很快就會找到工作，沒想到好幾次面試後，都沒拿到工作。雖然現在每個人都說男女應該平等，可是女大學畢業生找工作往往比男生困難得多，因為不少單位擔心婦女結婚以後生孩子會影響工作。蘭蘭覺得很不公平。她想："要是幾年前哥哥能有上大學的機會，我去開出租車，那多好啊。"

(SIMPLIFIED)

　　兰兰今年夏天大学毕业了。她有个哥哥，比她大两岁，高中毕业后没考上大学，就去开出租车了。兰兰的学习成绩比哥哥好，高中毕业后考进了一所名牌大学。她的父母薪水都不高，所以哥哥挣的钱差不多都给兰兰付学费了。好不容易等到兰兰大学毕业了，大家都以为她很快就会找到工作，没想到好几次面试后，都没拿到工作。虽然现在每个人都说男女应该平等，可是女大学毕业生找工作往往比男生困难得多，因为不少单位担心妇女结婚以后生孩子会影响工作。兰兰觉得很不公平。她想："要是几年前哥哥能有上大学的机会，我去开出租车，那多好啊。"

Questions (True/False):

( )　**1.**　Lanlan was a better student than her brother in high school.

( )　**2.**　Lanlan went to university, whereas her brother became a taxi driver.

( )　**3.**　Lanlan's brother helped her pay for her tuition.

( )　**4.**　Lanlan's family had anticipated that it would be difficult for Lanlan to find a job.

Questions (Multiple Choice):

( )　**5.**　According to the passage, what is the primary reason that some employers are reluctant to hire female college graduates?

    a. They don't believe that female college graduates are as capable as their male counterparts.

    b. They are unwilling to offer the same salary to a female college graduate as to a male college graduate.

    c. They are concerned that female college graduates will eventually let their families affect the quality of their work.

( )　**6.**　Which of the following statements is the most accurate?

    a. Lanlan has decided to join her brother as a taxi driver.

    b. Lanlan wishes that she could exchange positions with her brother.

    c. Lanlan believes that her brother deserved an opportunity to enter college.

2.

(TRADITIONAL)

中國在歷史上是個重男輕女的社會。雖然最近幾十年，婦女的家庭地位和社會地位都有了很大的提高，可是有些地方還有重男輕女的現象。比如在農村，不少夫妻希望生男孩，不想要女孩，結果中國的男孩比女孩多。這是一個很大的問題，中國政府要想出好辦法才能解決。但是我覺得這可能也是一件好事兒。為什麼呢？因為中國社會重男輕女的情況很快就要發生大變化了。你想，再過十幾年到二十年，現在五、六歲的孩子要結婚的時候，很多男的都會擔心找不到妻子。這樣，誰還能重男輕女啊？

(SIMPLIFIED)

中国在历史上是个重男轻女的社会。虽然最近几十年，妇女的家庭地位和社会地位都有了很大的提高，可是有些地方还有重男轻女的现象。比如在农村，不少夫妻希望生男孩，不想要女孩，结果中国的男孩比女孩多。这是一个很大的问题，中国政府要想出好办法才能解

决。但是我觉得这可能也是一件好事儿。为什么呢？因为中国社会重
男轻女的情况很快就要发生大变化了。你想，再过十几年到二十年，
现在五、六岁的孩子要结婚的时候，很多男的都会担心找不到妻子。
这样，谁还能重男轻女啊？

Questions (True/False):

( ) **1.** According to the writer, the problem of gender inequality is deeply rooted in Chinese history.

( ) **2.** According to the writer, the improvement in women's status over the last few decades has completely reversed in recent years.

( ) **3.** The writer assumes that the problem of gender imbalance in the population is largely confined to the upcoming generation.

( ) **4.** The writer believes that the status of Chinese women will be significantly improved in the next two decades.

Questions (Multiple Choice):

( ) **5.** Which of the following is considered the primary reason for the imbalance between boys and girls?

　a. the preference for boys in many families

　b. the difficulty young men have in finding women to marry

　c. the side effect of the government policy

( ) **6.** Which of the following best summarizes the perspective of the passage?

　a. It is shocking that some people in today's China still consider men superior to women.

　b. It is mind-boggling that there should be so many more boys than girls in today's China.

　c. It is ironic that the gender imbalance in the population could mean a great opportunity for improving women's status.

D. Look at the following sign and answer the questions. (INTERPRETIVE/PRESENTATIONAL)

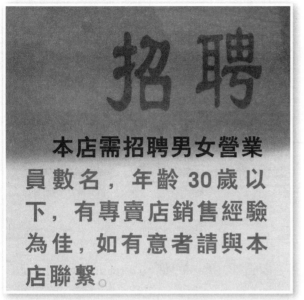 

本店需招聘男女營業員數名，年齡 30 歲以下，有專賣店銷售經驗為佳，如有意者請與本店聯繫。

本店需招聘男女营业员数名，年龄30岁以下，有专卖店销售经验为佳，如有意者请与本店联系。

1. 這份工作什麼人可以申請？

這份工作什麼人可以申請？

_____

2. 你對這份工作有興趣嗎？ 為什麼？

你对这份工作有兴趣吗？ 为什么？

_____

IV. Writing and Grammar Exercises

A. Building Characters

Form a character by combining the given components as instructed. Then write a word, a phrase, or a short sentence in which that character appears.

1. 上邊一個"田"，下邊一個"力氣"的"力"，

上边一个"田"，下边一个"力气"的"力"，

是 _____ 的 _____ 。

2. 左邊一個"酉"，右邊一個"加州"的"州"，

左边一个"酉"，右边一个"加州"的"州"，

是 _____ 的 _____ 。

3. 上邊一個"火", 下邊一個"火",

上边一个"火", 下边一个"火",

是 ＿＿＿＿＿＿＿＿＿的＿＿＿＿＿＿。

4. 上邊一個"自己"的"自", 下邊一個"心情"的"心",

上边一个"自己"的"自", 下边一个"心情"的"心",

是 ＿＿＿＿＿＿＿＿＿的＿＿＿＿＿＿。

5. 左邊一個人字旁, 右邊一個"言",

左边一个人字旁, 右边一个"言",

是 ＿＿＿＿＿＿＿＿＿的＿＿＿＿＿＿。

B. Convince others of why things are what they are by using 畢竟/毕竟 to introduce an obvious reason that speaker A may have overlooked.

EXAMPLE:

A: 爺爺最近老是忘這忘那的, 今天早上又忘了吃藥。

爷爷最近老是忘这忘那的, 今天早上又忘了吃药。

(He is 80 years old.)

→ **B:** 爺爺畢竟已經80歲了。

爷爷毕竟已经80岁了。

1. **A:** 這件衣服怎麼這麼貴?

这件衣服怎么这么贵?

(It's a name brand.)

→ **B:** ＿＿＿＿＿＿＿＿＿＿＿＿＿＿＿＿＿＿＿＿＿＿＿＿＿

2. **A:** 剛才舅舅看到我, 幾乎不認識我了。

刚才舅舅看到我, 几乎不认识我了。

(He hasn't seen you ever since you graduated from high school.)

→ **B:** ＿＿＿＿＿＿＿＿＿＿＿＿＿＿＿＿＿＿＿＿＿＿＿＿＿

3. **A:** 叔叔踢足球踢得太棒了, 跟職業球員差不多。

叔叔踢足球踢得太棒了, 跟职业球员差不多。

(He's played the sport for ten years.)

→ **B:** ＿＿＿＿＿＿＿＿＿＿＿＿＿＿＿＿＿＿＿＿＿＿＿＿＿

4. A: 阿姨的薪水真高，可能是他們公司最高的吧！

阿姨的薪水真高，可能是他们公司最高的吧！

(She's been working there since the company started.)

→ **B:** _____

C. Affirm A's statement using the 是…的 construction.

EXAMPLE:

A: 我相信有一天男女會平等。你說呢？

我相信有一天男女会平等。你说呢？

→ **B:** 我同意，<u>我相信有一天男女是會平等的</u>。

<u>我同意，我相信有一天男女是会平等的</u>。

1. A: 我認為工廠的困難能解決，你呢？

我认为工厂的困难能解决，你呢？

→ **B:** _____

2. A: 我覺得他們夫妻二人的感情會越來越好，你覺得呢？

我觉得他们夫妻二人的感情会越来越好，你觉得呢？

→ **B:** _____

3. A: 這種湯很有營養。你說呢？

这种汤很有营养。你说呢？

→ **B:** _____

4. A: 世界各種職業比賽都很公平，對吧？

世界各种职业比赛都很公平，对吧？

→ **B:** _____

D. Based on the texts in the lessons, introduce an example by using 拿…來說/拿…来说.

EXAMPLE:

Students who have scholarships also work at part-time jobs.

→ <u>有獎學金的學生也打工。拿麗莎來说吧，她就打工。</u>
<u>有奖学金的学生也打工。拿丽莎来说吧，她就打工。</u>

1. Many American-born Chinese students study Chinese.

→ _____

2. Some people think there is a lot of garbage online.

→ _____

3. Some people love buying souvenirs at tourist sites.

→ _____

4. Many couples in China don't want any children.

→ _____

E. Rewrite the following sentences using the "adjective+得+不得了" structure.

EXAMPLE:

雪梅舅舅的英文非常非常好。

雪梅舅舅的英文非常非常好。

→ 雪梅舅舅的英文好得不得了。

雪梅舅舅的英文好得不得了。

1. 那家飯館的菜很鹹很鹹。

那家饭馆的菜很咸很咸。

→ _____

2. 中國除夕夜非常非常熱鬧。

中国除夕夜非常非常热闹。

→ _____

3. 這個古城保留中國特色的建築很多很多。

这个古城保留中国特色的建筑很多很多。

→ _____

4. 雪梅的舅舅對舅媽非常非常體貼。

雪梅的舅舅对舅妈非常非常体贴。

→ _____

5. 放假的時候，中國各大旅遊景點都擠得很。

放假的时候，中国各大旅游景点都挤得很。

→ _____

F. Convert the following fractions into Chinese.

EXAMPLE: 1/10 → 十分之一

1. 1/2 → _____

2. 2/3 → _____

3. 7/8 → _____

4. 100/100 → _____

G. You and the main characters of the text are going to travel together, so you divide up the tasks of preparing for the trip. First match each person with his or her task and then declare who will be handling what by using 由.

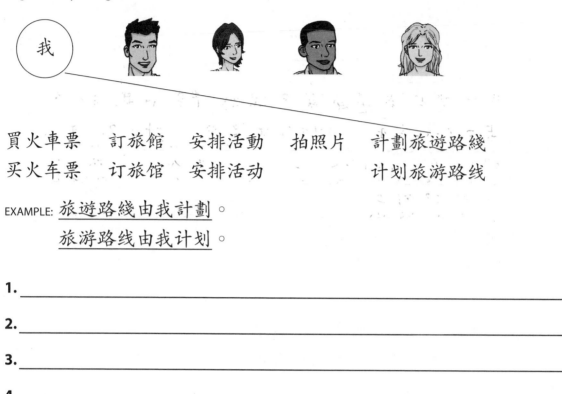

買火車票　　訂旅館　　安排活動　　拍照片　　計劃旅遊路綫
买火车票　　订旅馆　　安排活动　　　　　　　计划旅游路线

EXAMPLE: <u>旅遊路綫由我計劃</u>。
　　　　　<u>旅游路线由我计划</u>。

1. _____

2. _____

3. _____

4. _____

H. Translate the following dialogues into Chinese. (PRESENTATIONAL)

1. **A:** I heard some company bought a women's soccer team. It seems women's soccer is gradually gaining popularity.

   B: Right! After all, there are more and more women playing and watching the sport.

   听说一个企业买了一个女足队。看起来女足逐渐越来越有趣。对，毕竟，越来越多的妇女在看和踢足球。

2. **Salesperson:** What would you like to buy?

   Li Zhe:　　　Next month is my niece's birthday. I'd like to buy her a present.

   Salesperson: How old is she?

   Li Zhe:　　　She'll be nine next month.

   Salesperson: How about this panda (stuffed animal)? It's 40% off.

   Li Zhe:　　　Ever since she was in elementary school, my niece has loved playing soccer. I'll buy her a new soccer ball, then.

   Salesperson: But she's a girl, after all.

Li Zhe: What you're saying is unfair. Are you telling me girls can't play soccer? This is a gender-equal society.

Salesperson: Sir, I'm sorry. I didn't mean it that way. You can get a soccer ball on the second floor.

你想买什么?下个月是我侄女的生日,想给她买礼物。她多大?下个月会九岁。这个熊猫呢?打七个折。她从小学喜欢踢足球,给她买足球吧。毕竟她是女性的。你说得不公平意思是女孩子不能踢足球吧?这是一个男女平等的社会。对不起,不是我的意思。足球在二楼买得到。

3. **A:** Who will win today's soccer game? The Brazilian team or the Italian team?

B: Both of those teams used to be world champions. I think the score will be 0-0.

A: But recently the Brazilian team hasn't been performing well. They've been losing all the time. I think the Italian team will probably win.

今天的足球赛谁会赢?巴西队还是意大利队?那两个一前都是世界冠军,觉得比分会是零比零。可是最近巴西队成绩得不好,每次都输,觉得意大利队会赢。

4. A: Yesterday I was watching a soccer final match with your brother at his house. (Meanwhile) your sister-in-law was doing all the housework. Is your older brother a little bit of male chauvinist?

B: No, my brother is a model husband. He only can seem a little sexist when there is a soccer game on TV. Did you know my sister-in-law is a lawyer? She and my brother only have a daughter. My brother stays at home to take care of the daughter, cook, do dishes, and tidy up the house (while) my sister-in-law works.

昨天我跟你的哥哥在他的家看足球冠军赛,那时候你的嫂子把家务全做。你的哥哥表现大男子主义吗?哥哥是一个模范丈夫,只电视上有足球赛的时候才表现一点大男子主义。你知道嫂子是律师吗?她跟哥哥就有一个女孩子。我哥哥待在家做饭,洗碗,整理房子,嫂子工作。

I. Translate the following passages into Chinese. (PRESENTATIONAL)

1. Historically, Chinese society favored men over women. Many parents wanted boys. Girls didn't have the opportunity to be educated. Women's family and social status was also lower than men's. The situation changed greatly after 1949. Especially in the cities, women all began to work. Today China has many female doctors and teachers. However, China still has the phenomenon of gender inequity. For example, in the countryside girls have fewer opportunities to receive education than boys. Generally speaking, women's income is also lower than men's.

在历史上,中国是一个重男轻女的社会。很多父母要男孩子,女孩子没有教育机会。妇女的家庭和社会地位比男性的低得多。情况一九四九年以后就变得多了。特别在大城市里,女性的人都工作了。现在中国有很多女性的医生和老师,不过,中国还有男女不平等的现象。比如,农村的女孩子的教育机会比男孩子的少。一般,妇女的收入也比男人的低。

2. Gao Ming's (高明) sister-in-law's name is Wang Wenyin (王文音). She is an immigrant from Hong Kong. After marriage, she became Gao Wang Wenyin. Gao Ming asked Xuemei if women in mainland China (中國大陸／中国大陆) also use their husbands' family names after marriage. Xuemei said they didn't. Neither would she if she gets married. She would still be called Lin Xuemei. Xuemei asked if Gao Ming's brother was a bit chauvinist, and Gao Ming said no. He said women adopting their husbands' last names is a social practice (社會習慣／社会习惯) in Hong Kong. His brother is actually a model husband. Except for occasional disagreements about their children's education, his brother and sister-in-law are very affectionate toward each other, and that they are very considerate of each other, and take care of each other. The two are very equal at home.

高明的嫂子叫王文音，从香港族民来的。结婚子以后，成为了高王文音。高明问雪梅在中国大陆妇女会不会用丈夫的性。雪梅不会，舵也不会，还会是叫林雪梅。雪梅问高明他的哥哥是不是表现大男子主义，高明说不是。她说用丈夫的性是一个香港的社会习惯，哥哥本来是个模范丈夫。除了有时候在孩子的教育上不同意，感情很好，体贴一起，家庭的地位平等的。

J. Explain your views on whether men and women are equal in your community. You can include observations you have made in environments such as the family, school, workplace, and other social settings. (PRESENTATIONAL)

K. Storytelling (PRESENTATIONAL)

Write a story in Chinese based on the four cartoons below. Make sure that your story has a beginning, a middle, and an end. Also make sure that the transition from one picture to the next is smooth and logical.

1

2

3

4

Let's Review (LESSONS 11–15)

I. How Good Is Your Pronunciation?

Write down the correct pronunciation and tones of the following short sentences in *pinyin*, and use a recording device or computer to record them. Hand in the recording to your teacher if asked. Then translate each sentence into English. (INTERPRETIVE)

1. 學期結束了，大家決定繼續留在學校。
　 学期结束了，大家决定继续留在学校。

_____

_____

2. 吃年夜飯別忘了 "年年有餘" 這句話。
　 吃年夜饭别忘了 "年年有余" 这句话。

_____

_____

3. 中秋節是一家團圓的節日。
　 中秋节是一家团圆的节日。

_____

_____

4. 我的小學變化的確很大，讓我感覺有些陌生。
　 我的小学变化的确很大，让我感觉有些陌生。

_____

_____

5. 不是週末，旅遊景點竟擠滿了車，擠滿了遊客。
   不是周末，旅游景点竟挤满了车，挤满了游客。

---

6. 少數民族的建築和服裝都保留了很多傳統特色。
   少数民族的建筑和服装都保留了很多传统特色。

---

7. 無論是在硬臥還是軟臥車廂，我都睡得着。
   无论是在硬卧还是软卧车厢，我都睡得着。

---

8. 我從來不喜歡自助遊，都是參加旅行團。
   我从来不喜欢自助游，都是参加旅行团。

---

9. 高牆上掛著紅燈籠，氣氛特別好。
   高墙上挂着红灯笼，气氛特别好。

---

10. 排隊買門票看熊貓的遊客非常多。
    排队买门票看熊猫的游客非常多。

---

11. 那對退休夫妻早晨常在公園散步，偶爾也打打太極拳。

那对退休夫妻早晨常在公园散步，偶尔也打打太极拳。

---

12. 熬夜的人必須補充睡眠，注意飲食，否則容易生病。

熬夜的人必须补充睡眠，注意饮食，否则容易生病。

---

13. 大家都相信世界經濟會逐漸變好。

大家都相信世界经济会逐渐变好。

---

14. 請注意發音：是"妻管嚴"，而不是"氣管炎"。

请注意发音：是"妻管严"，而不是"气管炎"。

---

15. 網上有消息說中國女足贏了世界冠軍。

网上有消息说中国女足赢了世界冠军。

II. Put Your Chinese to Good Use! (PRESENTATIONAL)

Imagine that you are traveling to China. Before you go, find out if you know enough Chinese to deal with these situations:

A. Suppose a Chinese family invites you to spend Chinese New Year with them. What would you say at the New Year's Eve dinner? List your ideas here:

_____

_____

_____

_____

_____

_____

_____

B. Suppose you are touring a Chinese city that has gone through a lot of transformations. What things would you say to express your astonishment about the contrast between the old and the new? List your ideas here:

_____

_____

_____

_____

_____

_____

_____

C. Suppose you want to tell your Chinese friends about your impression of a famous tourist site you've just visited. What aspects would you touch upon? List your ideas here:

_____

_____

_____

_____

_____

_____

_____

D. Suppose you are interested in peoples' dietary habits and workout routines. What would you say to your Chinese friends about the similarities and differences between what you see in China and what you see in your own country? List your ideas here:

_____

_____

_____

_____

_____

_____

_____

_____

E. Suppose you meet a group of young professionals who wish to learn about equal rights in the workplace in your country. What points would you bring up in explaining the situation back home? List your ideas here:

_____

_____

_____

_____

_____

_____

_____

_____

III. Getting to Know China Better! (PRESENTATIONAL)

Make personalized lists in Chinese of the customs and places you have learnt about.

A. List a few things that Chinese people do to celebrate Chinese New Year. Rank these New Year's customs according to how much they appeal to you, with #1 as your favorite.

1. _____

2. _____

3. _____

4. _____

5. _____

B. List the things that you have learned about Nanjing. Rank them according to how they impress you, with #1 as the most memorable.

1. _____

2. _____

3. _____

4. _____

5. _____

C. List the facts that you have learned about traveling in Yunnan. Rank them according to how useful they are to you, with #1 as the most interesting.

1. _____

2. _____

3. _____

4. _____

5. _____

D. List the exercises that you would like to participate in when you go to China. Rank them according to how eager you are to take part in them, with #1 as the one you want to do the most.

1. _____

2. _____

3. _____

4. _____

5. _____

E. List the facts you have learned about gender roles in Chinese society. Rank them according to how interesting they were to you, with #1 as the most surprising.

1. _____

2. _____

3. _____

4. _____

5. _____

IV. Express Yourself! (PRESENTATIONAL)

Based on, but not limited to, the information you have provided in Parts II and III, present an oral report or write a short essay in Chinese in response to each of the following questions.

A. Suppose you are going to host a Chinese New Year party. How would you prepare and decorate for the occasion? What would you say and offer to your guests?

B. Suppose you are going to make a documentary on the rise or decline of a town or city. What kinds of sights and sounds would reflect the changes? How would you dramatically present and narrate these changes?

C. Suppose you are organizing your own tour to Yunnan. What route would you choose, what places would you visit, and what do you need to know about those places?

D. Suppose you are a personal trainer. What would you say to encourage your clients to have healthier eating and exercise habits?

E. Suppose you are being interviewed by a Chinese graduate student in sociology about gender equality in your home country. What would you say about the general attitudes toward gender relations in your country, and what examples would you give to support your arguments?

第十六課　環境保護與節約能源
第十六课　环境保护与节约能源

I. Listening Comprehension

A. Textbook Content (INTERPRETIVE)

Listen to the recording for the Textbook and answer the questions in English.

1. Why did Zhang Tianming and his friends decide to go mountain climbing?

一个月没见面了,更没机会接近大自然。

2. What transportation did they take to get to the foot of the mountain? Why?

骑自行车,不贵,也不挤,能锻炼身体

3. According to Lisa, what are the Chinese government's regulations on the use of heating and air conditioning in offices and other public places?

规定不让冬天不能超不二十摄氏度,夏天不能少于二十六度。

4. What has recently changed in restaurants with regard to the use of chopsticks?

比较多的人自己带筷子。

5. Why do people now have to bring their own bags when shopping at supermarkets?

如果不带的话,超市让他们买塑料袋,不免费。

6. According to Zhang Tianming and his friends, what should people start doing in their daily lives to support environmental protection?

要随手关灯,节约用水,少开车,多骑车,多走路。

B. Workbook Dialogue (INTERPRETIVE)

Listen to the recording for the Workbook and answer the questions.

Questions (True/False):

(F) **1.** The woman is calling from her car.

(T) **2.** When the woman went shopping she hadn't heard about the new policy at the supermarket.

(T) **3.** The man sounds supportive of the new policy at the supermarket.

(F) **4.** The woman asks the man to help carry the groceries as they are too heavy.

(F) **5.** The man decides not to drive because he doesn't think the woman really needs his help.

C. Workbook Narratives (INTERPRETIVE)

Listen to the recording for the Workbook and answer the questions in English.

1. Questions:

a. What job offer did the speaker receive?

_____

b. What dilemma is the speaker facing?

_____

c. What is the purpose of this message?

_____

d. If you were Little Lin, what advice would you offer the speaker?

_____

2. Questions:

a. What do you think is the relationship between the speaker and Xiaoming?

_____

b. What had happened that triggered this speech?

_____

c. How would you summarize the speaker's message?

_____

D. Workbook Listening Rejoinder (INTERPERSONAL)

In this section, you will hear two people talking. After hearing the first speaker, select the best from the four possible responses given by the second speaker.

_____

II. Speaking Exercises

A. Practice asking and answering the following questions. (INTERPERSONAL)

1. 你住的地方空氣污染嚴重嗎？為什麼？

你住的地方空气污染严重吗？为什么？

2. 你住的城市垃圾回收的工作順利嗎？為什麼？

你住的城市垃圾回收的工作顺利吗？为什么？

3. 除了爬山、騎自行車以外，你覺得還有什麼樣的活動有益於身體健康？

除了爬山、骑自行车以外，你觉得还有什么样的活动有益于身体健康？

B. Practice speaking on the following topics. (PRESENTATIONAL)

1. 請談談你平常為環保做些什麼。

请谈谈你平常为环保做些什么。

2. 請談談你平常怎麼節能。

请谈谈你平常怎么节能。

3. The Chinese government has imposed regulations on the use of heating and air conditioning in public places. Do you think your government should come up with similar laws? Why or why not?

III. Reading Comprehension

A. Building Words

Complete this section by writing the characters, the *pinyin*, and the English equivalent of each new word formed. Guess the meaning before you use a dictionary to confirm.

1. "資料" 的 "資" ＋ "能源" 的 "源"

"资料" 的 "资" ＋ "能源" 的 "源"

→ ＿＿＿＿＿　＿＿＿＿＿　＿＿＿＿＿

　　　　　new word　　*pinyin*　　English

2. "有益" 的 "益" ＋ "好處" 的 "處"

"有益" 的 "益" ＋ "好处" 的 "处"

→ ＿＿＿＿＿　＿＿＿＿＿　＿＿＿＿＿

3. "漂亮" 的 "亮" ＋ "美麗" 的 "麗"

"漂亮" 的 "亮" ＋ "美丽" 的 "丽"

→ ＿＿＿＿＿　＿＿＿＿＿　＿＿＿＿＿

4. "太陽" 的 "陽" + "農曆" 的 "曆"

    "太阳" 的 "阳" + "农历" 的 "历"

    → _____ _____ _____

5. "身體" 的 "體" + "溫度" 的 "溫"

    "身体" 的 "体" + "温度" 的 "温"

    → _____ _____ _____

B. Match the verb with its appropriate object. Note that some of the verbs can be matched with more than one object. For this exercise, use the combinations that have been taught in the lessons so far.

1. 減輕/减轻	a. 污染
2. 保護/保护	b. 能源
3. 省	c. 特色
4. 減少/减少	d. 環境/环境
5. 保留	e. 負擔/负担
6. 節約/节约	f. 錢/钱

C. Read the passages and answer the questions. (INTERPRETIVE)

1.

(TRADITIONAL)

改革開放以來，中國經濟發展得非常快，但是也造成了嚴重的環境污染。中國政府現在越來越重視環保問題了。一個辦法是節約能源。政府已經規定，公共場所夏天空調的溫度不能太低，冬天暖氣的溫度不能太高。另外一個辦法是利用太陽能和風能。很多中國家庭都用太陽能熱水器，又省錢，又不污染環境。要是你坐火車去中國西部，可能會看到一個個風力發電站。很多人認為，中國很快就會成為利用太陽能和風能最多的國家。

(SIMPLIFIED)

改革开放以来，中国经济发展得非常快，但是也造成了严重的环境污染。中国政府现在越来越重视环保问题了。一个办法是节约能源。政府已经规定，公共场所夏天空调的温度不能太低，冬天暖气的温度不能太高。另外一个办法是利用太阳能和风能。很多中国家庭都用太阳能热水器，又省钱，又不污染环境。要是你坐火车去中国西部，可能会看到一个个风力发电站。很多人认为，中国很快就会成为利用太阳能和风能最多的国家。

Questions (True/False):

( ) **1.** The writer considers the environmental damage in China a negative result of the country's rapid economic development.

( ) **2.** According to the writer, the Chinese government pays more attention to environmental protection now than it did before.

( ) **3.** All households in China have to follow the government's rules on heating and air conditioning.

( ) **4.** The writer is pessimistic about the prospect of environmental protection in China.

Questions (Multiple Choice):

( ) **5.** According to the passage, which statement is the most accurate?

   a. China is the country that has the richest solar and wind energy resources.

   b. China is becoming the country that will be making more use of solar and wind energy than any other country.

   c. China will be the first country whose economy will be driven mostly by solar and wind energy.

2.

(TRADITIONAL)

哥哥：

　　我現在已經不在原來那家公司上班了。在那裏，我的工作就是賣一次性筷子給日本和美國，給公司賺了很多錢，所以我的薪水也很不錯。可是我每次拿薪水的時候，都要問自己：為了那些一次性筷子，我們砍了多少樹啊？我的不少同學都在做環保工作，做有益於環境保護的事，可是我為了賺錢，總做對環境沒有好處的事。我這樣一想，晚上就睡不著覺了，最後我決定不去那家公司上班了。你們不用為我擔心，我會找到新的工作的。我現在找工作的標準是，不管薪水多少，一定是要有益於環保的。

妹妹

(SIMPLIFIED)

哥哥：

　　我现在已经不在原来那家公司上班了。在那里，我的工作就是卖一次性筷子给日本和美国，给公司赚了很多钱，所以我的薪水也很不错。可是我每次拿薪水的时候，都要问自己：为了那些一次性筷子，我们砍了多少树啊？我的不少同学都在做环保工作，做有益于环境保护的事，可是我为了赚钱，总做对环境没有好处的事。我这样一想，晚上就睡不着觉了，最后我决定不去那家公司上班了。你们不用为我担心，我会找到新的工作的。我现在找工作的标准是，不管薪水多少，一定是要有益于环保的。

妹妹

Questions (True/False):

( ) **1.** The writer is currently unemployed.

( ) **2.** The company that the writer worked for was engaged in a lucrative export business.

( ) **3.** The writer made a lot of money for the company but was not paid well.

( ) **4.** The writer had to work the night shift frequently and didn't get enough sleep.

Questions (Multiple Choice):

( ) **5.** Which of the statements is the most accurate?

　　　a. The writer was curious about how many trees her company had cut down.

　　　b. The writer felt guilty that her company had cut down many trees.

　　　c. The writer marveled that her company had cut down so many trees.

( ) **6.** How did the writer feel when she thought about her former classmates?

　　　a. She was ashamed that she was doing something the opposite of what they were doing.

　　　b. She was glad that she was doing something similar to what they were doing.

　　　c. She was indifferent to whether they were doing similar things or not.

( ) **7.** What can be said about the writer's next job?

　　　a. It will be a well-paid and environmentally friendly job.

　　　b. It will be an environmentally friendly job with a low salary.

　　　c. It will be an environmentally friendly job, and the salary could be high or it could be low.

D. Look at the signs and answer the questions. (INTERPRETIVE/PRESENTATIONAL)

1.

請把這個商店的名字翻譯成英文：
请把这个商店的名字翻译成英文：_____

2.

請用英文寫出它讓你做什麼：
请用英文写出它让你做什么：_____

3.

這個人的英文翻譯好不好？為什麼？
这个人的英文翻译好不好？为什么？

_____

4.

What's everyone's duty? Answer in English: _____

E. Read the ad and answer the questions.

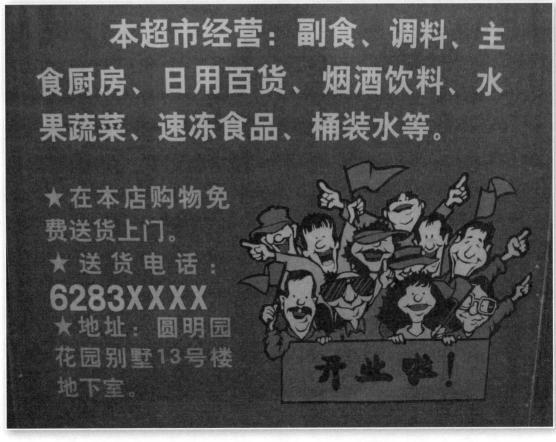

1. 廣告上說他們賣什麼東西？請寫出四種，並翻譯成英文。

广告上说他们卖什么东西？请写出四种，并翻译成英文。

_____

2. 他們還有什麼服務讓你覺得在那兒買東西很方便？請用英文寫出來。

他们还有什么服务让你觉得在那儿买东西很方便？请用英文写出来。

_____

IV. Writing and Grammar Exercises

A. Building Characters

Form a character by combining the given components as instructed. Then write a word, a phrase, or a short sentence in which that character appears.

1. 左邊一個三點水，右邊一個"原來"的"原"，

左边一个三点水，右边一个"原来"的"原"，

是 _____ 的 _____ 。

2. 左邊一個提手旁，右邊一個"佳"，

左边一个提手旁，右边一个"佳"，

是 _____ 的 _____ 。

3. 左邊一個"耳"，右邊一個"又"，

左边一个"耳"，右边一个"又"，

是 _____ 的 _____ 。

4. 左邊一個"夫子廟"的"夫"，右邊一個"見面"的"見"，

左边一个"夫子庙"的"夫"，右边一个"见面"的"见"，

是 _____ 的 _____ 。

5. 左邊一個"石頭"的"石"，右邊一個"欠錢"的"欠"，

左边一个"石头"的"石"，右边一个"欠钱"的"欠"，

是 _____ 的 _____ 。

B. Based on the clues given, use "V1 的 V1, V2 的 V2" to describe the scenes.

EXAMPLE: quiet in a library

  圖書館裏，人們看書的看書，睡覺的睡覺，很安靜。
   图书馆里，人们看书的看书，睡觉的睡觉，很安静。

1. bustling activity in front of the Temple of Confucius

→ _____

2. vitality in a park

 → _____

3. joy on the soccer field after winning a championship

→ _____

C. Contemplate different alternatives using ···吧···吧.

EXAMPLE:

A: 你打算怎麼去聽音樂會?

你打算怎么去听音乐会?

→ **B:** <u>坐出租車吧, 太貴, 走路吧, 太遠, 我還是騎自行車去吧</u>。
<u>坐出租车吧, 太贵, 走路吧, 太远, 我还是骑自行车去吧</u>。

1. A: 你今天想買什麼水果?

你今天想买什么水果?

→ **B:** _____ 。

2. A: 你週末想做什麼?

你周末想做什么?

→ **B:** _____ 。

3. A: 小白明天過生日, 你準備送什麼禮物?

小白明天过生日, 你准备送什么礼物?

→ **B:** _____ 。

D. Fill in the blanks with 想起(來)/想起(来) or 想出(來)/想出(来).

1. 我們去年是什麼時候去爬山的？你＿＿＿＿＿＿了嗎？

我们去年是什么时候去爬山的？你＿＿＿＿＿＿了吗？

2. 大家還不知道怎麼給爺爺過八十歲生日，希望能趕快

＿＿＿＿＿＿一個好主意。

大家还不知道怎么给爷爷过八十岁生日，希望能赶快

＿＿＿＿＿＿一个好主意。

3. 她的手機號碼你＿＿＿＿＿＿以後，請告訴我。

她的手机号码你＿＿＿＿＿＿以后，请告诉我。

4. 柯林＿＿＿＿＿＿一個去長城的好辦法，又省錢又好玩兒。

柯林＿＿＿＿＿＿一个去长城的好办法，又省钱又好玩儿。

5. 叔叔在哪個企業單位工作我到現在還沒＿＿＿＿＿＿。

叔叔在哪个企业单位工作我到现在还没＿＿＿＿＿＿。

E. First, match each activity with its possible benefit.

1. 運動/运动	**a.** 環境保護/环境保护
2. 利用太陽能或風能/ 利用太阳能或风能	**b.** 減少白色污染/ 减少白色污染
3. 不隨便亂扔垃圾/ 不随便乱扔垃圾	**c.** 身體健康/ 身体健康
4. 不用塑料袋	**d.** 節約傳統能源/ 节约传统能源

Then, based on each match, make a statement using 有益於/有益于.

1. ＿＿＿＿＿＿

2. ＿＿＿＿＿＿

3. ＿＿＿＿＿＿

4. ＿＿＿＿＿＿

F. Convert the following into Chinese using 於/于.

EXAMPLE: 3 > 2   →   <u>三大於二/三大于二</u>。

1. 8 < 9   →   _____

2. 101 > 100   →   _____

3. 2/3 > 1/2   →   _____

4. 79 + 24 = 103   →   _____

5. 1000 − 438 = 562   →   _____

EXAMPLE: today   Beijing 15°C   Nanjing 19°C

→   <u>北京今天的温度低於南京</u>。
<u>北京今天的温度低于南京</u>。

6. tonight   Shenzhen 27°C   Tianjin 21°C   → _____

7. tomorrow   Shanghai 20°C   Hangzhou 22°C   → _____

8. yesterday   New York 70°F   Harbin 16°C   → _____

G. Complete the following sentences using V著V著/V着V着.

EXAMPLE:

→   <u>天明看電視，看著看著就睡着了</u>。
<u>天明看电视，看着看着就睡着了</u>。

1. → 馬克爬山，
马克爬山，_____。

2. → 柯林吃魚，
   柯林吃鱼，_____。

3. → 麗莎聽故事，
   丽莎听故事，_____。

H. Translate the following dialogue into Chinese. (PRESENTATIONAL)

A: Your shirt is really beautiful. Where did you get it?

B: It's an old shirt of my mom's. I got my furniture at a second-hand furniture store (舊傢具店/旧家具店), too.

A: You are really thrifty.

B: I'm still paying back my student loan. I don't have a lot of money. Besides, I feel that if old things are still usable, why buy new ones? Now I try my best to buy as few things as possible and waste as little as possible.

A: No wonder you are thrifty with paper, too.

B: If we don't conserve and don't pay attention to recycling, the earth will have more and more trash.

A: I agree.

你的衬衫非常漂亮，在哪买的？
是我妈的久衬衫，我的家具也在旧家具店买的。你很节约。
我还偿还学生贷款，钱不多。在说，我觉得久的东西还能用为什么要买新的呢？现在我尽可能少买东西少浪费。
可见你跟纸也很节约。如果我们不节约不注意回收，世界上的垃圾就会越来越多。我同意。

I. Translate the following passages into Chinese. (PRESENTATIONAL)

1. "Protect the earth; protect our home." We will meet Thursday evening at 7:00 in Room 305 in Building No. 5 to discuss how environmental protection (can) start with small things and start with each and every one of us. We welcome everybody to participate (in the meeting).

保护世界,保护家庭。我们周四七点在五号楼房间三零五讨论怎么环保可能从小地方做,从每个人做起。我们请问大家参加。

2. "We love green. We don't love white." Let's protect the green earth and reduce white pollution together. Please conserve paper, do not use disposable chopsticks, do not drink bottled water. This weekend we will go to the outskirts of the city to plant trees (種樹／种树) and recycle plastic bags and plastic bottles. We welcome everybody to participate.

我们爱绿,不爱白。我们一起保护绿色世界,减少白污染。请节约纸,不用一次性的筷,不喝瓶装水。这个周末去市外种树,回收塑料袋和塑料水瓶。请大家参加。

3. My cousin Tianliang (天亮) used to bike to work. Now he has started to drive. However, his girlfriend Xiaoyin (小音) feels that riding a bike can not only strengthen the body but also save money. Furthermore, it is good for the environment. That's why she doesn't want to buy a car. She says that since he bought a car, Tianliang seldom exercises and has put on weight. Besides, the streets are crowded with cars. Driving is not as convenient as biking. Tianliang feels that what Xiaoyin says makes sense. He plans to sell his car, buy a bicycle, and bike to work with Xiaoyin.

我的表哥以前骑车上班,现在开始开车了。结果他的女朋友觉骑车又锻炼身体,又省钱。在说对环境好。所她不想买车。她说因为天亮买了车,所以他很少锻炼,也胖起来了。天亮觉得小音的说法有道理,打算卖车,买自行车,跟小音骑车上班。

4. Tianming's email message to his father

Dad,

  Yesterday my friends and I biked out of town to hike in the mountains. We saw many houses using solar energy to generate electricity. We thought it was really cool. After I got back to the dorm in the evening, I went online and did some research. It turns out that many places in China use solar and wind power. Now many countries in the world are like China, suffering from an energy crisis. If they continue to use coal and oil, the consequences will be too much to contemplate. But solar and wind power are inexhaustible, and will help the world solve the energy crisis.

Tianming

爸爸：昨天我跟朋友一起出城市爬山。我们见了很多用太阳能的房子，很酷。我晚上回宿舍以后上网研究了。结果很多地方在中国用太阳能和风能。现在很多国家像中国，闹能危机。如果继续用煤和石油，后果会不堪设想，可是太阳能和风能都是取之不尽，可以解决世界的能危机。

天明。

J. What lifestyle changes are people in your community making to protect the environment? Compile your observations as a report titled 《綠色生活/绿色生活》.(PRESENTATIONAL)

K. Storytelling (PRESENTATIONAL)

Write a story in Chinese based on the four cartoons below. Make sure that your story has a beginning, a middle, and an end. Also make sure that the transition from one picture to the next is smooth and logical.

1

2

3

4

第十七課　　理財與投資
第十七課　　理財与投资

I. Listening Comprehension

A. Textbook Content (INTERPRETIVE)

Listen to the recording for the Textbook and answer the questions in English.

1. Why have many Chinese people started considering investment methods other than savings accounts?

房价涨得很快。

2. What are the different views on financial investment mentioned in the text?

有些人全给女子受到最好的教育, 也有人消费享受。

3. Originally, what was Zhang Tianming's aunt's plan for her personal savings?

省吃俭用给孙子孙女上大学。

4. Why didn't Zhang Tianming's cousin and his fiancée agree to his aunt's suggestion of buying a new car?

他会用一辆就可以。

5. Did Zhang Tianming's aunt buy a new apartment as planned? Why or why not?

买了因为表哥跟她说会为姑妈的贷款。

6. If your aunt were in a similar situation, and she would like to get your opinion, what would you tell her?

我会跟她说一样的。

B. Workbook Dialogue (INTERPRETIVE)

Listen to the recording for the Workbook and answer the questions.

Questions (True/False):

(F) **1.** The man made some money in the stock market in the past, but not this time.

(T) **2.** The man is somewhat emotional because of his investment results.

(F) **3.** The man wanted to invest in the stock market because he was very wealthy.

(T) **4.** The woman seems to know the stock market better than the man.

( ) **5.** According to the woman, it is now the best time to sell stocks.

( ) **6.** According to the woman, the current situation in the stock market will not necessarily last long.

C. Workbook Narratives (INTERPRETIVE)

Listen to the recording for the Workbook and answer the questions in English.

1. Questions:

a. What do you think is the relationship between the speaker and the person she is speaking to?

b. What is the speaker's preferred way of managing money? Why?

c. What investment did the other person make a few months ago? How has the return been?

d. Is the speaker worried? Why or why not?

2. Questions:

a. Why does the speaker have to leave this voicemail for Daliang?

b. How do the speaker and his wife plan to pay for their new apartment?

c. Is the speaker sure that he and his wife will sign the contract next week? Why or why not?

d. What does the speaker want Daliang to do?

D. Workbook Listening Rejoinder (INTERPERSONAL)

In this section, you will hear two people talking. After hearing the first speaker, select the best from the four possible responses given by the second speaker.

II. Speaking Exercises

A. Practice asking and answering the following questions. (INTERPERSONAL)

1. 你認為什麼樣的投資風險高？

你认为什么样的投资风险高？

2. 你認為怎樣理財沒有風險？ 為什麼？

你认为怎样理财没有风险？ 为什么？

3. 你認為父母需要為子女將來的教育費擔心嗎？ 為什麼？

你认为父母需要为子女将来的教育费担心吗？ 为什么？

B. Practice speaking on the following topics. (PRESENTATIONAL)

1. 請談談如果你有一百萬元，你會怎麼投資。

请谈谈如果你有一百万元，你会怎么投资。

2. 你贊成省吃儉用地過日子，還是以"錢只有花了才是自己的"的態度過日子？ 為什麼？

你赞成省吃俭用地过日子，还是以"钱只有花了才是自己的"的态度过日子？ 为什么？

3. Recap the story from the textbook about the two elderly women, and explain the moral of the story. Do you agree or disagree with that message? Why?

III. Reading Comprehension

A. Building Words

Complete this section by writing the characters, the *pinyin*, and the English equivalent of each new word formed. Guess the meaning before you use a dictionary to confirm.

1. "炒股"的"炒" + "方便麵"的"麵"

"炒股"的"炒" + "方便面"的"面"

→ _____ _____ _____

            new word   *pinyin*   English

2. "鬱悶"的"悶" + "生氣"的"氣"

"郁闷"的"闷" + "生气"的"气"

→ _____ _____ _____

3. "辛苦"的"苦" + "用功"的"功"

→ _____ _____ _____

4. "簽合同" 的 "簽" + "名字" 的 "字"
    "签合同" 的 "签" + "名字" 的 "字"

    →   _____   _____   _____

5. "突然" 的 "突" + "變化" 的 "變"
    "突然" 的 "突" + "变化" 的 "变"

    →   _____   _____   _____

B. Fill in the blanks with the words provided.

(TRADITIONAL)

討論   興趣   反對   危機   注意

1. 旁邊的幾個朋友正在分享自己投資理財的經驗，這引起小王的_____。
2. 導遊的建議，有些人贊成，但也引起某些人的_____。
3. 在安靜的病房裏，突然有人的腳步聲，引起了醫生的_____。
4. 煤和石油越來越少，如果再不節能，恐怕會引起全世界的能源_____。
5. 張教授希望用報上的文章來引起大家對環保問題的_____。

(SIMPLIFIED)

讨论   兴趣   反对   危机   注意

1. 旁边的几个朋友正在分享自己投资理财的经验，这引起小王的_____。
2. 导游的建议，有些人赞成，但也引起某些人的_____。
3. 在安静的病房里，突然有人的脚步声，引起了医生的_____。
4. 煤和石油越来越少，如果再不节能，恐怕会引起全世界的能源_____。
5. 张教授希望用报上的文章来引起大家对环保问题的_____。

C. Read the passages and answer the questions. (INTERPRETIVE)

1.

(TRADITIONAL)

　　白先生和白太太夫妻倆收入很高。以前他們一直把錢存在銀行裏，安全是安全，可是錢增加得太慢，於是他們開始考慮用別的方式投資。白先生認為買房子好，可是白太太覺得炒股賺錢更快。他們誰也說服不了誰，只好用一半錢買了一套房子，把另一半錢放進股市裏。從那以後，夫妻倆一直鬧彆扭。房價漲的時候，白先生就說：“要是我們不買股票，買兩套房子，那多好啊。”股票漲的時候，白太太就說：“要是我們不買房子，把錢都用來買股票，那多好啊。”上個月，他們把房子和股票都賣了，把錢又存到銀行裏去了。現在，他們的錢漲得很慢，可是兩個人不再鬧彆扭了。

(SIMPLIFIED)

　　白先生和白太太夫妻俩收入很高。以前他们一直把钱存在银行里，安全是安全，可是钱增加得太慢，于是他们开始考虑用别的方式投资。白先生认为买房子好，可是白太太觉得炒股赚钱更快。他们谁也说服不了谁，只好用一半钱买了一套房子，把另一半钱放进股市里。从那以后，夫妻俩一直闹别扭。房价涨的时候，白先生就说：“要是我们不买股票，买两套房子，那多好啊。”股票涨的时候，白太太就说：“要是我们不买房子，把钱都用来买股票，那多好啊。”上个月，他们把房子和股票都卖了，把钱又存到银行里去了。现在，他们的钱涨得很慢，可是两个人不再闹别扭了。

Questions (True/False):

( ) **1.** In the past, Mr. and Mrs. Bai managed to have bank savings despite their low income.

( ) **2.** Mr. and Mrs. Bai agreed with each other to withdraw their money from the bank, but disagreed with each other on how to invest it.

( ) **3.** Mr. and Mrs. Bai were at odds with each other when their investments did not generate good returns.

( ) **4.** Mr. and Mrs. Bai would say now that depositing their money in the bank is not a bad way to invest it after all.

Questions (Multiple Choice):

( ) **5.** Which of the following best describes the Bais' way of investing until last month?

    a. They invested half their money in real estate and the other half in stocks.

    b. They invested all their money in real estate half of the time and then in stocks the other half of the time.

    c. They received half of their returns from their real estate investment and the other half from their stocks.

( ) **6.** Based on the passage, which of the following is most accurate?

    a. Both the real estate market and the stock market were stagnant.

    b. Both real estate prices and stock prices were extremely volatile.

    c. Both the real estate market and the stock market had their high points, but at different times.

( ) **7.** In the end Mr. and Mrs. Bai decided to go back to bank savings because _____.

    a. the growth of their bank savings was slow but very steady

    b. bank savings happened to be a good compromise for them

    c. neither of them was an aggressive investor

2.

(TRADITIONAL)

表姐：

　　你告訴我你這幾年賺了不少錢，我真的非常高興。聽舅舅舅媽說，你小時候他們收入不高，連給你買雙新鞋的錢都沒有。現在不一樣了。你們有了大房子，也有了新車，還有了不少存款。我同意你說的，把錢存在銀行裏並不是最好的理財方式。我知道舅舅舅媽一直想再買一套房子，等到房價漲的時候再賣出去。我也知道你自己覺得股票市場賺錢可能更容易。可是，除了房子和股市以外，難道就沒有別的投資方式了嗎？在你們家過春節的時候，我就注意到，你們那兒很多老年人早上在公園裏打太極拳，可是年輕人並沒有很多鍛煉身體的地方。所以我覺得，花錢開個健身房一定受歡迎，也一定會賺錢。我有個朋友在廣州開健身房。要是你有興趣，我可以讓他跟你聊聊。

小靜

(SIMPLIFIED)

表姐：

你告诉我你这几年赚了不少钱，我真的非常高兴。听舅舅舅妈说，你小时候他们收入不高，连给你买双新鞋的钱都没有。现在不一样了。你们有了大房子，也有了新车，还有了不少存款。我同意你说的，把钱存在银行里并不是最好的理财方式。我知道舅舅舅妈一直想再买一套房子，等到房价涨的时候再卖出去。我也知道你自己觉得股票市场赚钱可能更容易。可是，除了房子和股市以外，难道就没有别的投资方式了吗？在你们家过春节的时候，我就注意到，你们那儿很多老年人早上在公园里打太极拳，可是年轻人并没有很多锻炼身体的地方。所以我觉得，花钱开个健身房一定受欢迎，也一定会赚钱。我有个朋友在广州开健身房。要是你有兴趣，我可以让他跟你聊聊。

小静

Questions (True/False):

( ) **1.** Xiaojing's cousin cannot afford to buy a pair of new shoes because all her money is in the bank.

( ) **2.** Xiaojing is happy to report that she has made a lot of money in recent years.

( ) **3.** Xiaojing and her cousin agree that saving money in the bank is not the best form of investment.

( ) **4.** Xiaojing's uncle and aunt hope to buy another apartment because they don't like the one they currently live in.

( ) **5.** Xiaojing's cousin prefers to invest in the stock market because she thinks it gives a better return than the real estate market.

( ) **6.** Xiaojing promises to spend the next Chinese New Year with her cousin's family.

Questions (Multiple Choice):

( ) **7.** How are Xiaojing and her cousin related?

    a. Xiaojing's mother is the sister of her cousin's mother.

    b. Xiaojing's father is the brother of her cousin's father.

    c. Xiaojing's maternal grandparents are her cousin's paternal grandparents.

( ) **8.** Why does Xiaojing recommend that her cousin open a gym as a way of investing?

    a. because both the stock market and the real estate market are sluggish

    b. because she thinks that a new gym would be popular and profitable

    c. because her cousin's city is very close to Guangzhou

D. Look at the ad and answer the question in Chinese or English. (INTERPRETIVE/PRESENTATIONAL)

這個廣告能引起你投資買房的興趣嗎？為什麼？

这个广告能引起你投资买房的兴趣吗？为什么？

E. This is a blank deposit receipt for a bank in China. Imagine you have just made a deposit at the bank. Use this form to fill in your name, account number (012345), the amount that you have deposited (1000), the currency that you have deposited (RMB), and the fee (10) that the bank has charged you. (INTERPRETIVE/PRESENTATIONAL)

戶　名				客户回單
賬戶/卡號				
種　類				
幣　別		鈔(匯)		
存　期		起息日		
存款金額：			元	
手續費：			元	
流水號：				
			銀行簽章	

戶　名				客户回單
賬戶/卡号				
种　类				
币　别		鈔(汇)		
存　期		起息日		
存款金额：			元	
手续费：			元	
流水号：				
			银行签章	

IV. Writing and Grammar Exercises

A. Building Characters

Form a character by combining the given components as instructed. Then write a word, a phrase, or a short sentence in which that character appears.

1. 左邊一個三點水，右邊一個"緊張"的"張"，
左边一个三点水，右边一个"紧张"的"张"，
是 ＿＿＿＿＿＿＿的＿＿＿＿ 。

2. 左邊一個"火車站"的"火"，右邊一個"減少"的"少"，
左边一个"火车站"的"火"，右边一个"减少"的"少"，
是 ＿＿＿＿＿＿＿的＿＿＿＿ 。

3. 外邊一個"出門"的"門"，裏邊一個"心事"的"心"，
外边一个"出门"的"门"，里边一个"心事"的"心"，
是 ＿＿＿＿＿＿＿的＿＿＿＿ 。

4. 左邊一個提手旁，右邊一個"贊成"的"贊"，
左边一个提手旁，右边一个"赞成"的"赞"，
是 ＿＿＿＿＿＿＿的＿＿＿＿ 。

5. 上邊一個"相信"的"相"，下邊一個"心情"的"心"，
上边一个"相信"的"相"，下边一个"心情"的"心"，
是 ＿＿＿＿＿＿＿的＿＿＿＿ 。

B. Fill in the blanks with 一向 or 一直.

1. 小王上大學以來，＿＿＿＿＿＿在理財公司實習。
小王上大学以来，＿＿＿＿＿＿在理财公司实习。

2. 知道自己這個學期的成績後，小王＿＿＿＿＿＿很鬱悶。
知道自己这个学期的成绩后，小王＿＿＿＿＿＿很郁闷。

3. 小王＿＿＿＿＿＿怎麼說就怎麼做，所以大家都很相信他。
小王＿＿＿＿＿＿怎么说就怎么做，所以大家都很相信他。

4. 小王昨天晚上手機＿＿＿＿＿＿關機，害得同學找不到他。
小王昨天晚上手机＿＿＿＿＿＿关机，害得同学找不到他。

5. 小王＿＿＿＿＿＿＿十分注意自己的生活習慣與飲食健康。

小王＿＿＿＿＿＿＿十分注意自己的生活习惯与饮食健康。

C. Twins often share things. These twin sisters are no exception. Based on the visual clues, write sentences using 合.

EXAMPLE:

→   她們姐妹合租一套公寓。

她们姐妹合租一套公寓。

1.

→ ＿＿＿＿＿＿＿＿＿＿＿＿＿＿＿＿＿＿＿＿＿＿＿＿＿＿＿＿＿＿

2.

→ ＿＿＿＿＿＿＿＿＿＿＿＿＿＿＿＿＿＿＿＿＿＿＿＿＿＿＿＿＿＿

3.

→ ＿＿＿＿＿＿＿＿＿＿＿＿＿＿＿＿＿＿＿＿＿＿＿＿＿＿＿＿＿＿

4.

→ ＿＿＿＿＿＿＿＿＿＿＿＿＿＿＿＿＿＿＿＿＿＿＿＿＿＿＿＿＿＿

D. Based on the information given, state how the characters are finally rewarded for their patience.

Example: learned tai chi

➔ <u>麗莎學太極拳學了很長時間，終於學會了</u>。
   <u>丽莎学太极拳学了很长时间，终于学会了</u>。

1.   found a suitable job

➔ _____

2.   prepared/was ready for her graduate school exam

➔ _____

3.   found his keys

➔ _____

4.   climbed to the top of the mountain

➔ _____

E. Based on the clues, complete the mini-dialogues using 接著/接着.

EXAMPLE: **A:** 這個字我已經寫了一百遍了，可以了吧？
          这个字我已经写了一百遍了，可以了吧？

➔   **B:** <u>接著寫，再寫一百遍</u>。
          <u>接着写，再写一百遍</u>。

1.A: 這個錄音我已經聽了半個鐘頭了，能休息一下嗎？
       这个录音我已经听了半个钟头了，能休息一下吗？

➔ **B:** _____

2.A: 這個瑜伽動作我練了五次了，換一個動作，行嗎？

這个瑜伽动作我练了五次了，换一个动作，行吗？

→ **B:** _____

3.A: 這個景點的照片我拍了二十幾張了，夠了吧？

这个景点的照片我拍了二十几张了，够了吧？

→ **B:** _____

4.A: 這些舊衣服我們已經扔了十幾件了，剩下的難道不能送人？

这些旧衣服我们已经扔了十几件了，剩下的难道不能送人？

→ **B:** _____

F. Word Association

EXAMPLE: 我們可以在圖書館做什麼？

我们可以在图书馆做什么？

→ 我們可以在圖書館看書、借書、看報、上網、休息等等。

我们可以在图书馆看书、借书、看报、上网、休息等等。

1. 我們可以上網做什麼？

我们可以上网做什么？

→ _____

2. 我們可以去銀行做什麼？

我们可以去银行做什么？

→ _____

G. Using 把, ask someone to finish the following tasks.

1. Open the window.

→ _____

2. Turn off the light.

→ _____

3. Finish your tea.

→ _____

4. Wash your cup (clean).

→ _____

5. Tidy up your room.

→ _____

6. Get the dinner ready.

→ _____

H. Translate the following dialogues into Chinese. (PRESENTATIONAL)

1. A: Which stocks have been going up lately?

   B: Now everybody takes environmental protection very seriously. If you don't want to flip stocks for the short term, but would like to invest over the long term (長期/长期), I think that buying solar and wind power–related stocks is not a bad idea.

为什么股市最近涨得？

现在人完全都注意保护世界。如果你不想短期买股票，可是想长期买，最好买太阳能和风能有关的股票。

2. A: Did you know that there is an economist (經濟學家/经济学家) who opened a bank and lends money to women who don't have any money because he feels that women know how to manage and spend money?

   B: No, I have never heard of such a bank.

   A: He also lends money to women who don't have any money because he wants to improve women's social status. He is coming to school this evening to tell us about (介紹/介绍) his ideas. We can listen together.

你知道有一个经济学家开了一个银行把钱借给妇女因为他觉得妇女知道怎么理财。

我没听过。他也给没有钱的妇女借钱，想提高妇女的社会地为。他今天来学校介绍他的主意，我们可以一起听。

_____

3. A: I'd like to ask some money-management questions, is that possible?

   B: No problem. May I ask how old you are?

   A: Twenty-five.

   B: I think you can buy some stocks. Although the stock market sometimes goes down and it's risky to buy stocks, you are not flipping stocks for the short term, so it won't be a big problem. If you have already retired, it's best to keep your money in the bank.

A: What about buying a house? Some people say that buying a house is also a good investment.

B: If it's the house that you live in, it doesn't count as an investment. It would indeed be a good investment if you bought a house and rented it out.

A: Thanks. I'll go home and think about it.

我想问一些理财的问题，可以吗？没问题，请问你几岁？二十五岁。我觉你可以买股票，虽然股市会跌，也有风险，但是你不是短期买，不大的问题。如果以经退休了，是好钱放在银行里。买房子呢？有人说买房子也是好的投资。如果是你住的那儿，就不算投资，如是租的就是好的投资。xiexie，我会回家想一想。

I. Translate the following passages into Chinese. (PRESENTATIONAL)

1. My cousin sold his car. He also made some money flipping stocks, so he'd like to buy a house. He has his eye on a three-bedroom, one-living-room, and two-bathroom house, only it's outside the city and rather inconvenient to get to work. His fiancée says, "Houses in the city are too expensive. It's difficult to take out a loan. Monday through Friday we can live with my parents or yours. On weekends we can bike to the suburbs (and stay there). Besides, in the future there's bound to be a subway. If we don't buy now, when housing prices go up, we won't have any more opportunities."

我表哥买了他的车，也挣了钱买股票，所以想买房子。他想买一套三房，一厅，两卫的房子，可是在城市外上班有一点麻烦。他的未婚妻说"城里的房太贵，拿贷款太难。星期一到五可以跟你的或者我的父母住。周末可以骑车到城市外住。在说地铁肯定会有。如果现在不买，房价涨的时候，机会享没了。

2. Li Wen's parents worked for more than thirty years, and are finally retired. They have always been very frugal (with food and other expenses), so they have some savings in the bank. They feel that although money accumulates very slowly in the bank, it's the safest. They don't like flipping stocks. Li Wen thinks that if you have money you should spend and enjoy it. Although she has very little savings, she often flips stocks. She says houses are too expensive now. If she doesn't flip stocks and make some money, she won't have enough money to buy a house. Her parents see that she sometimes makes money and sometimes loses money. They are concerned. Occasionally, they clash with each other because of Li Wen's flipping stocks.

李文的父母工作了廿多年，终于退休了。他们一向很省吃俭用，所以银行里有些存款。他们觉得虽然钱在银行里很慢的攒，是安全，不喜欢买股票。李文觉得有钱的话应该消费享受。虽然她钱不多，她常常买股票。她说房子太贵，如果不买股票，就没有钱买房子。父母看她有时候赔钱，担心！有时候他们会吵架。

J. Write down your short-term and long-term financial goals. Describe how you can achieve those goals and how long it may take to reach them. When you set your goals, you should take into consideration things such as student loans, living expenses, how to be financially responsible, how to be a smart investor, what parts of life are most important to you, etc. (PRESENTATIONAL)

K. Storytelling (PRESENTATIONAL)

Write a story in Chinese based on the four cartoons below. Make sure that your story has a beginning, a middle, and an end. Also make sure that the transition from one picture to the next is smooth and logical.

第十八課　中國歷史

第十八課　中国历史

 # I. Listening Comprehension

A. Textbook Content (INTERPRETIVE)

Listen to the recording for the Textbook and answer the questions in English.

1. Why did Lisa and her friends want to visit the museum?

他们对中国历史有兴趣。

2. What does Li Wen think about Confucius's place in Chinese history?

孔子是中国最重要的一位教育家。

3. How would you summarize the merits and faults of the First Emperor?

他修了长城和宫殿，可是也杀了很多人。

4. Why are the Han and Tang dynasties considered among the most powerful dynasties in Chinese history?

汉朝中国开始跟外国贸易，唐朝对中国文化，经济，教育都很重要。

5. Can you name China's Four Great Inventions?

中国最有名的发明是造纸，火药，指南针，和活字印刷。

6. What happened in 1911 that overthrew the last dynasty in Chinese history?

孙中山领导了一个革命。

B. Workbook Dialogue (INTERPRETIVE)

Listen to the recording for the Workbook and answer the questions.

Questions (True/False):

(T) **1.** The woman seems to know more about Chinese history than the man.

(T) **2.** According to the woman, the First Emperor was the most famous emperor in all of Chinese history.

(T) **3.** According to the woman, the First Emperor did both good things and bad things.

(T) **4.** According to the woman, the scholars whom the First Emperor killed had all made great contributions.

(T) **5.** The man seems to assume that a famous emperor should be a good emperor.

(T) **6.** As the woman sees it, a historic figure didn't have to be good in order to be famous.

C. Workbook Narratives (INTERPRETIVE)

Listen to the recording for the Workbook and answer the questions in English.

1. Questions:

a. Is Lisa going to visit the museum tomorrow afternoon? Why or why not?

_____

b. Who would like to visit the museum with Lisa and Li Wen? Why?

_____

c. What is the purpose of this message?

_____

2. Questions:

a. Who is the speaker? What is the purpose of this message?

_____

b. According to the speaker, how does the Chinese National Museum compare to other world museums?

_____

c. What is the speaker's suggestion regarding Lisa's planned tour of the museum?

_____

d. Has the number of visitors to the museum increased or decreased recently? According to the speaker, what could be the reason?

_____

D. Workbook Listening Rejoinder (INTERPERSONAL)

In this section, you will hear two people talking. After hearing the first speaker, select the best from the four possible responses given by the second speaker.

_____

II. Speaking Exercises

A. Practice asking and answering the following questions. (INTERPERSONAL)

1. 孔子為什麼偉大？

孔子为什么伟大？

2. 秦始皇為什麼有名？

秦始皇为什么有名？

3. 唐朝在中國歷史上為什麼重要？

唐朝在中国历史上为什么重要？

B. Practice speaking on the following topics. (PRESENTATIONAL)

1. 請談談中國哪一個朝代給你的印象最深。

请谈谈中国哪一个朝代给你的印象最深。

2. 請談談了解一個國家的歷史為什麼重要。

请谈谈了解一个国家的历史为什么重要。

3. Describe the typical view of the First Emperor's reign.

III. Reading Comprehension

A. Building Words

Complete this section by writing the characters, the *pinyin*, and the English equivalent of each new word formed. Guess the meaning before you use a dictionary to confirm.

1. "偉大" 的 "偉" + "事業" 的 "業"

"伟大" 的 "伟" + "事业" 的 "业"

→ ＿＿＿＿＿　＿＿＿＿＿　＿＿＿＿＿

　　　　　　new word　　*pinyin*　　English

2. "建立" 的 "建" + "國家" 的 "國"

"建立" 的 "建" + "国家" 的 "国"

→ ＿＿＿＿＿　＿＿＿＿＿　＿＿＿＿＿

3. "展廳" 的 "展" + "遊覽" 的 "覽"

"展厅" 的 "展" + "游览" 的 "览"

→ ＿＿＿＿＿　＿＿＿＿＿　＿＿＿＿＿

4. "皇帝"的"皇" + "宫殿"的"宫"

   "皇帝"的"皇" + "宫殿"的"宫"

               →   _____ _____ _____

5. "修长城"的"修" + "管理"的"理"

   "修长城"的"修" + "管理"的"理"

               →   _____ _____ _____

B. Fill in the blanks with 參觀/参观 or 遊覽/游览.

(TRADITIONAL)

1. 明天有一個外國人要來_____我們的工廠，請大家做好準備。

2. 石林的石頭千奇百怪，我們一邊_____，一邊聽導遊給我們講跟石頭有關的故事。

3. _____博物館的時候，千萬別隨便亂拍照。

4. 坐船從東往西_____長江，感覺非常特別。

5. 我們想_____一下你們建築公司在城東蓋的那棟大樓，不知道方便不方便？

6. 聽説有個老外坐飛機到北京_____各個有名的烤鴨店。

(SIMPLIFIED)

1. 明天有一个外国人要来_____我们的工厂，请大家做好准备。

2. 石林的石头千奇百怪，我们一边_____，一边听导游给我们讲跟石头有关的故事。

3. _____博物馆的时候，千万别随便乱拍照。

4. 坐船从东往西_____长江，感觉非常特别。

5. 我们想_____一下你们建筑公司在城东盖的那栋大楼，不知道方便不方便？

6. 听说有个老外坐飞机到北京_____各个有名的烤鸭店。

C. Read the passages and answer the questions. (INTERPRETIVE)

1.

(TRADITIONAL)

　　漢朝的時候中國就開始跟西方進行貿易了。那時候中國人把很多絲綢送到西方去賣，所以那條貿易來往的路就叫做"絲綢之路"。除了絲綢以外，中國人還賣給西方人很多茶。後來，中國人開始從海上跟西方進行貿易，所以又有了"海上絲綢之路"。有一些西方國家最早的茶是從"絲綢之路"買到的，另一些西方國家最早的茶是從"海上絲綢之路"買到的。很有意思的是，在這兩種國家的語言裏，"茶"的發音是不一樣的。跟"絲綢之路"有關的國家，"茶"的發音和中國北方話裏"茶"的發音差不多。跟"海上絲綢之路"有關的國家，"茶"的發音跟中國東南沿海一帶"茶"的發音差不多。

(SIMPLIFIED)

　　汉朝的时候中国就开始跟西方进行贸易了。那时候中国人把很多丝绸送到西方去卖，所以那条贸易来往的路就叫做"丝绸之路"。除了丝绸以外，中国人还卖给西方人很多茶。后来，中国人开始从海上跟西方进行贸易，所以又有了"海上丝绸之路"。有一些西方国家最早的茶是从"丝绸之路"买到的，另一些西方国家最早的茶是从"海上丝绸之路"买到的。很有意思的是，在这两种国家的语言里，"茶"的发音是不一样的。跟"丝绸之路"有关的国家，"茶"的发音和中国北方话里"茶"的发音差不多。跟"海上丝绸之路"有关的国家，"茶"的发音跟中国东南沿海一带"茶"的发音差不多。

Questions (True/False):

( ) **1.** The writer suggests that the Chinese started making silk during the Han Dynasty.

( ) **2.** Despite the name "Silk Road," silk was not the only commodity in China's early trade with the West.

( ) **3.** Concurrent with the Silk Road, China opened another sea route for trade with the West.

( ) **4.** The writer suggests that the "Maritime Silk Road" started from the coastal area of southern China.

Questions (Multiple Choice):

( ) **5.** According to the writer, how was tea introduced to the West?

    a. It was brought to the West along the Silk Road.

    b. It was brought to the West wrapped in silk fabric.

    c. It was brought to the West along the Silk Road as well as in ships.

( ) **6.** According to the writer, how are the pronunciations of the word for tea in different Western languages historically related to the introduction of tea from China?

    a. The pronunciations were determined by the earliest tea merchants from different Western countries.

    b. The pronunciations were determined by the different types of tea that were preferred in different Western countries.

    c. The pronunciations were determined by the geographic origins of the different routes for tea trade.

2.

(TRADITIONAL)

A: 哎，老王，要是讓你選，你最願意做中國哪個朝代的人？

B: 我最願意當唐朝人。因為唐朝的時候，中國是統一的國家，經濟和人民生活都發展到比較高的水平，在很多方面都是世界最先進的。我想我不用擔心找不到工作。

A: 我以為你是對唐詩有興趣呢。

B: 我知道唐詩特別有名。我讀過李白的詩，可是不大懂。

A: 要是你看到李白，想跟他說些什麼？

B: 我會說：「李白先生，謝謝你對中國文化的偉大貢獻。」

A: 李白聽了一定會很高興。

B: 我雖然不懂李白的詩，可是我一定會成為李白的好朋友。等到我死了，我就請人把我的墳墓修在李白的墳墓旁邊。

A: 為什麼？

B: 這樣我的墳墓就成了有名的旅遊點了。

(SIMPLIFIED)

A: 哎，老王，要是让你选，你最愿意做中国哪个朝代的人？

B: 我最愿意当唐朝人。因为唐朝的时候，中国是统一的国家，经济和人民生活都发展到比较高的水平，在很多方面都是世界最先进的。我想我不用担心找不到工作。

A: 我以为你是对唐诗有兴趣呢。

B: 我知道唐诗特别有名。我读过李白的诗，可是不大懂。

A: 要是你看到李白，想跟他说些什么？

B: 我会说："李白先生，谢谢你对中国文化的伟大贡献。"

A: 李白听了一定会很高兴。

B: 我虽然不懂李白的诗，可是我一定会成为李白的好朋友。等到我死了，我就请人把我的坟墓修在李白的坟墓旁边。

A: 为什么？

B: 这样我的坟墓就成了有名的旅游点了。

Questions (True/False):

( ) **1.** Old Wang and his friend were born during the Tang Dynasty.

( ) **2.** Old Wang assumes that the unemployment rate must be low in an economically developed society with high living standards.

( ) **3.** Old Wang is an expert on all Tang poetry.

( ) **4.** Old Wang thinks that Li Bai made remarkable contributions to Chinese culture.

Questions (Multiple Choice):

( ) **5.** Which of the following is the most accurate description of Old Wang's imagined relationship with Li Bai?

    a. He would become Li Bai's friend in order to understand his poetry better.

    b. He would read Li Bai's poetry in order to become his friend.

    c. He believes that he would become Li Bai's friend without being able to understand his poetry.

( ) **6.** What does Old Wang say about his own tomb?

    a. He would like to be buried at a famous tourist site.

    b. He believes that his tomb would become a famous tourist site.

    c. He would let Li Bai decide where his tomb should be located.

D. Look at the sign and answer the question. (INTERPRETIVE)

這個牌子上少了一個英文字母，是什麼？請加上。

这个牌子上少了一个英文字母，是什么？请加上。

E. Look at the picture and answer the question in Chinese. (INTERPRETIVE/PRESENTATIONAL)

什麼東西壞了，可以來這兒修？

什么东西坏了，可以来这儿修？

F. Look at the information and answer the question in Chinese. (INTERPRETIVE/PRESENTATIONAL)

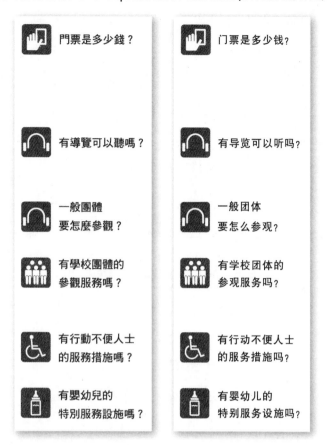

什麼人在什麼地方會問這些問題？
什么人在什么地方会问这些问题？

_____

IV. Writing and Grammar Exercises

A. Building Characters

Form a character by combining the given components as instructed. Then write a word, a phrase, or a short sentence in which that character appears.

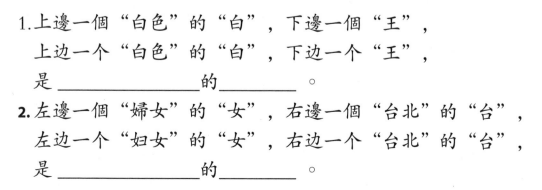

1. 上邊一個"白色"的"白"，下邊一個"王"，
   上边一个"白色"的"白"，下边一个"王"，
   是 _____的_____ 。

2. 左邊一個"婦女"的"女"，右邊一個"台北"的"台"，
   左边一个"妇女"的"女"，右边一个"台北"的"台"，
   是 _____的_____ 。

3. 上邊一個 "朝代" 的 "代"，下邊一個 "衣服" 的 "衣"，
   上边一个 "朝代" 的 "代"，下边一个 "衣服" 的 "衣"，
   是 ＿＿＿＿＿＿＿＿的＿＿＿＿＿ 。

4. 上邊一個 "工作" 的 "工"，下邊一個 "貝"，
   上边一个 "工作" 的 "工"，下边一个 "贝"，
   是 ＿＿＿＿＿＿＿＿的＿＿＿＿＿ 。

5. 上邊一個 "其中" 的 "其"，下邊一個 "土"，
   上边一个 "其中" 的 "其"，下边一个 "土"，
   是 ＿＿＿＿＿＿＿＿的＿＿＿＿＿ 。

B. First, match each person with the title he or she is associated with.

1. 孔子	**a.** 哲學家／哲学家
2. Aristotle	**b.** 畫家／画家
3. Thomas Edison	**c.** 教育家
4. Marie Curie	**d.** 文學家／文学家
5. Shakespeare	**e.** 發明家／发明家
6. Frida Kahlo	**f.** 科學家／科学家

Then describe each person's status in the world, using 之一.

EXAMPLE: 孔子是世界上最偉大的教育家之一。
孔子是世界上最伟大的教育家之一。

1. ＿＿＿＿＿＿＿＿＿＿＿＿＿＿＿＿＿＿＿＿＿＿＿＿＿＿＿＿＿＿＿＿ 。

2. ＿＿＿＿＿＿＿＿＿＿＿＿＿＿＿＿＿＿＿＿＿＿＿＿＿＿＿＿＿＿＿＿ 。

3. ＿＿＿＿＿＿＿＿＿＿＿＿＿＿＿＿＿＿＿＿＿＿＿＿＿＿＿＿＿＿＿＿ 。

4. ＿＿＿＿＿＿＿＿＿＿＿＿＿＿＿＿＿＿＿＿＿＿＿＿＿＿＿＿＿＿＿＿ 。

5. ＿＿＿＿＿＿＿＿＿＿＿＿＿＿＿＿＿＿＿＿＿＿＿＿＿＿＿＿＿＿＿＿ 。

C. Do some research online and complete the following sentences using 其中.

EXAMPLE: population

北京、上海、東京、紐約都是世界上的大城市，<u>其中東京的</u>
<u>人口最多</u>。

北京、上海、东京、纽约都是世界上的大城市，<u>其中东京的</u>
<u>人口最多</u>。

1. land area

北京、上海、東京、紐約都是世界上的大城市，

北京、上海、东京、纽约都是世界上的大城市，

_____。

2. consumption/cost of living

北京、上海、東京、紐約都是世界上的大城市，

北京、上海、东京、纽约都是世界上的大城市，

_____。

3. cost of housing

北京、上海、東京、紐約都是世界上的大城市，

北京、上海、东京、纽约都是世界上的大城市，

_____。

4. air pollution

北京、上海、東京、紐約都是世界上的大城市，

北京、上海、东京、纽约都是世界上的大城市，

_____。

D. First, match each person with the topic he or she knows more about than the others in the group.

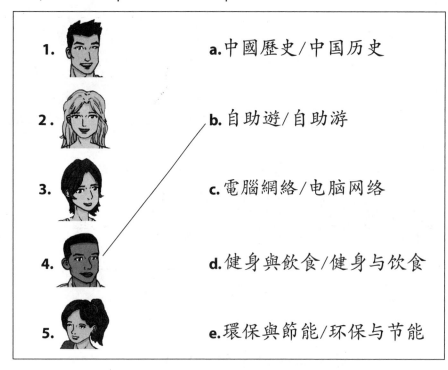

1.   **a.** 中國歷史／中国历史

2.   **b.** 自助遊／自助游

3.   **c.** 電腦網絡／电脑网络

4.   **d.** 健身與飲食／健身与饮食

5.   **e.** 環保與節能／环保与节能

Then state that fact in a sentence, using 在…方面.

EXAMPLE: 在自助遊方面，柯林比其他人都懂得多。
在自助游方面，柯林比其他人都懂得多。

1. _____ ○

2. _____ ○

3. _____ ○

4. _____ ○

E. Based on your own situation, answer the following questions by using "跟…有關(係)／跟… 有关(系)."

EXAMPLE: **A:** 你比較喜歡看哪方面的書？政治、經濟、文化還是歷史？
你比较喜欢看哪方面的书？政治、经济、文化还是历史？

→   **B:** 我比較喜歡看跟文化有關的書。
我比较喜欢看跟文化有关的书。

1. 你常常上網查哪方面的資料？股市，房價，購物，旅遊，還是天氣？

你常常上网查哪方面的资料？股市，房价，购物，旅游，还是天气？

→ **B:** _____ 。

2. 你比較注意哪方面的新聞？政治、經濟、社會還是國際？

你比较注意哪方面的新闻？政治、经济、社会还是国际？

→ **B:** _____ 。

3. 哪方面的事情更會引起你的重視？健身，環保，節能還是理財？

哪方面的事情更会引起你的重视？健身，环保，节能还是理财？

→ **B:** _____ 。

F. Based on the visual clues, state everyone's New Year's resolutions using 再也不.

EXAMPLE:

→ 柯林說從明年開始他再也不喝瓶裝水了。

柯林说从明年开始他再也不喝瓶装水了。

1.

→ _____

2.

→ _____

3.

→ _____

G. Translate the following dialogues into Chinese. (PRESENTATIONAL)

1. **A:** Tomorrow we'll have a test on Chinese history. Please go over the emperors of the Qing Dynasty this evening.

   B: What, Teacher, tomorrow we'll have a Chinese history test? We don't like tests or reviewing.

   A: Everybody knows that Confucius left us a lot of sayings. Among those, "Having friends from afar, isn't that a great joy!" is one of the most famous. There's another saying that is equally famous. That is, "Studying and frequently reviewing (學而時習之/学而时习之), isn't that a great joy!" I wish everyone a happy time this evening reviewing.

   明天我会有中国历史考试，请今天晚上学习秦朝的皇帝。啊，老师，明天有中国历史考试？我们不喜欢考试或者学习。大家知道孔子给了我们很多句话，其中"有朋自远方来，不亦乐乎"是最有名的之一。还有一句话一样有名，"学而时习之，不亦乐乎"。我希望大家晚上开心地学习。

2. **A:** Have you visited the Terracotta Warrior Museum?

   B: No, but I'd like to. I'm very interested in the First Emperor of the Qin Dynasty.

   A: The First Emperor is important in Chinese history, but many people don't like him because he killed many scholars. He also made many people build palaces and a tomb for him.

   B: Whether you like him or not, I think he was very influential for China's cultural development. For example, he unified the Chinese script.

   A: I agree with that. On the foundation of the Qin Dynasty, the Han Dynasty enabled China to make great strides politically and economically.

   你参观了兵马俑博物馆吗？没有，可是我很想参观。我对秦始皇很有心趣。秦始皇对中国历史很重要，但是很多人不喜欢他因为他杀了很多读书人。他也让了很人给他修宫殿和坟墓。如果你喜不喜欢他，我学得他对中国的文化发展很有影响。比方说，他把中文文字统一了。我同意，在秦朝的基础上，汉朝使中国在政治和经济都有很大的发展。

3. A: Let's go climb the Great Wall tomorrow. How about it?

B: Great. I've wanted to go for a long time, but I've never had the opportunity. I hear that the Great Wall's history is about two or three thousand years old. Construction of the Great Wall started before the Qin Dynasty.

A: That's right, but our history teacher says that most of the Great Wall that we see today was built during the Ming Dynasty (明朝).

B: How do we get there?

A: We can take the bus.

B: It's boring to take the bus. Let's bike there, shall we?

A: OK. It's a deal! Biking is not only cheap but also healthy.

我们明天去爬长城，好吧？好，我很久想去可是没有机会。我听说长城的历史两三千年久。长城是秦朝一前先修。对的，但我们的历史老师说我们现在看到的 到长城是明朝大多修的。我们怎么去呢？可以生公共汽车。那么无聊的，骑车去好吧？好吧，骑车又便宜又健康。

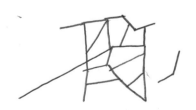

长城有两三千年的历史。

H. Translate the following passage into Chinese. (PRESENTATIONAL)

Confucius said, "Having friends visiting from afar, isn't that a great joy!" Welcome to Shandong (山東/山东), everyone. Confucius is the most important educator and thinker in Chinese history and had a great impact on China. Today there are Confucius Institutes the world over. Shandong is the birthplace of Confucius. The most famous temple of Confucius is right in Shandong. There are also many tourist sites in Shandong, for instance, Mount Tai (泰山). I hope that besides having lots of opportunities to practice Chinese in Shandong, everyone will also be able to climb Mount Tai. Finally, I'd like to give these T-shirts printed (印) with Confucius's words to everyone as a gift.

I. If you were asked to give a short talk on one Chinese dynasty, which one would you discuss? Explain your choice and draft your speech here. Don't forget to mention when the dynasty started and ended, how long the dynasty lasted, its significance in Chinese history, its most important figures, and their achievements. (PRESENTATIONAL)

J. Storytelling (PRESENTATIONAL)

Write a story in Chinese based on the four cartoons below. Make sure that your story has a beginning, a middle, and an end. Also make sure that the transition from one picture to the next is smooth and logical.

1
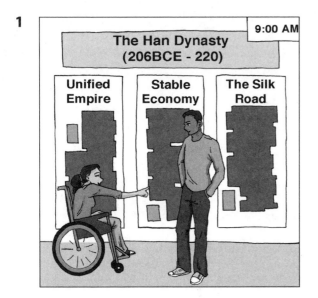

2

3
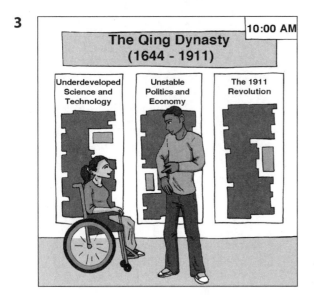

4

19

第十九課   面試

第十九课   面试

🔘 I. Listening Comprehension

A. Textbook Content (INTERPRETIVE)

Listen to the recording for the Textbook and answer the questions in English.

1. Why are people who return from overseas sometimes playfully called "sea turtles"?

_____

2. Why was Lin Xuemei nervous at the beginning of her interview?

_____

3. How did Xuemei convince the general manager that she had not returned to China because of a lack of success in America?

_____

4. Did Xuemei say that she wanted to work in Beijing in order to be with her boyfriend? Why or why not?

_____

5. What does Xuemei think is her own biggest weakness?

_____

6. Does Xuemei sound optimistic or pessimistic on the phone about her job interview? What are the reasons for her to feel that way?

_____

B. Workbook Dialogue (INTERPRETIVE)

Listen to the recording for the Workbook and answer the questions.

Questions (True/False):

( ) **1.** The woman says that the Chinese automobile industry started about twenty years ago.

( ) **2.** The Dadi Company builds automobiles that produce less pollution.

( ) **3.** The man is looking for a job in the automobile industry.

( ) **4.** The man believes that her company offers jobs with higher compensation than its competitors.

( ) **5.** According to the man, he likes the woman's company because of its profitable sales.

( ) **6.** The woman considers the man a true environmentalist.

Question:

If you were the woman, would you hire the man? Why or why not?

_____

C. Workbook Narratives (INTERPRETIVE)

Listen to the recording for the Workbook and answer the questions in English.

1. Questions:

a. What did the speaker do before she started job-hunting?

_____

b. Why did one of the companies that interviewed the speaker decide not to hire her?

_____

c. Is the speaker currently working for either of the companies that offered her a job? Why or why not?

_____

2. Questions:

a. Who do you think the speaker is? Who is Miss Zhang?

_____

b. What is the purpose of this speech?

_____

c. According to the speaker, what are Miss Zhang's credentials?

_____

d. Why is Miss Zhang familiar with the products and market of the speaker's company?

_____

D. Workbook Listening Rejoinder (INTERPERSONAL)

In this section, you will hear two people talking. After hearing the first speaker, select the best from the four possible responses given by the second speaker.

_____

II. Speaking Exercises (INTERPERSONAL)

A. Practice asking and answering the following questions.

1. 什麼樣的人被叫做 "海龜"?

什么样的人被叫做 "海龟"?

2. 你緊張的時候，怎麼讓自己輕鬆點兒?

你紧张的时候，怎么让自己轻松点儿?

3. 你覺得自己是不是一個善於安排時間的人? 請解釋。

你觉得自己是不是一个善于安排时间的人? 请解释。

B. Practice speaking on the following topics. (PRESENTATIONAL)

1. 請談談怎麼樣安排時間才能有益於學習或工作。

请谈谈怎么样安排时间才能有益于学习或工作。

2. 請談談你自己的優點與缺點。

请谈谈你自己的优点与缺点。

3. Xuemei managed to impress the general manager during the interview. If you had been in Xuemei's place, what would you have done? Explain why you would have handled the interview in a similar or different way.

III. Reading Comprehension

A. Building Words

Complete this section by writing the characters, the *pinyin*, and the English equivalent of each new word formed. Guess the meaning before you use a dictionary to confirm.

1. "西方" 的 "西" + "服裝" 的 "裝"

"西方" 的 "西" + "服装" 的 "装"

→ _____ _____ _____

           new word   *pinyin*   English

2. "濕" + "溫度" 的 "度"

"湿" + "温度" 的 "度"

→ _____ _____ _____

3. "嚴肅" 的 "肅" ＋ "安靜" 的 "靜"

"严肃" 的 "肃" ＋ "安静" 的 "静"

→ ＿＿＿＿＿＿ ＿＿＿＿＿＿ ＿＿＿＿＿＿

4. "陰轉多雲" 的 "陰" ＋ "太陽" 的 "陽"

"阴转多云" 的 "阴" ＋ "太阳" 的 "阳"

→ ＿＿＿＿＿＿ ＿＿＿＿＿＿ ＿＿＿＿＿＿

5. "解釋" 的 "解" ＋ "回答" 的 "答"

"解释" 的 "解" ＋ "回答" 的 "答"

→ ＿＿＿＿＿＿ ＿＿＿＿＿＿ ＿＿＿＿＿＿

B. Which of the following can only be filled in with 常常? Which ones can have either 常常 or 往往？

1. 經理告訴雪梅開始上班以後＿＿＿＿＿＿需要出國開會。

经理告诉雪梅开始上班以后＿＿＿＿＿＿需要出国开会。

2. 太極拳要打得好必須＿＿＿＿＿＿練習。

太极拳要打得好必须＿＿＿＿＿＿练习。

3. 我很喜歡參觀博物館，無論去哪個博物館，＿＿＿＿＿＿都得花好幾個小時的時間。

我很喜欢参观博物馆，无论去哪个博物馆，＿＿＿＿＿＿都得花好几个小时的时间。

4. 剛從大學畢業的人，沒有實習經驗，＿＿＿＿＿＿找不到工作。

刚从大学毕业的人，没有实习经验，＿＿＿＿＿＿找不到工作。

5. 面試人的人＿＿＿＿＿＿很嚴肅，一點都不幽默，甚至有點兒嚇人。

面试人的人＿＿＿＿＿＿很严肃，一点都不幽默，甚至有点儿吓人。

C. Read the passages and answer the questions. (INTERPRETIVE)

1.

(TRADITIONAL)

　　對於在西方國家大學裏學有所成的中國留學生來說，回中國好還是留在西方好？這是一個引起很多人思考的問題。不少中國留學生覺

得，回國找工作不是一個很容易的決定。為什麼呢？因為中國公司的
管理方式跟西方不完全一樣，他們擔心可能不太習慣。還有，中國的
環保是一個大問題，一些大城市的空氣質量不好。可是另外一些中國
留學生認為現在是回中國工作的好機會。為什麼呢？因為21世紀以來
中國的經濟發展是世界上最快的，現在是很多中國公司需要人材的時
候。加上中國留學生學習了西方的管理方式，又懂中國的文化，所以
一定會很受歡迎。我覺得這兩種看法都有道理，不過我相信從西方回
中國的"海龜"肯定會越來越多。

(SIMPLIFIED)

　　对于在西方国家大学里学有所成的中国留学生来说，回中国好还
是留在西方好？这是一个引起很多人思考的问题。不少中国留学生觉
得，回国找工作不是一个很容易的决定。为什么呢？因为中国公司的
管理方式跟西方不完全一样，他们担心可能不太习惯。还有，中国的
环保是一个大问题，一些大城市的空气质量不好。可是另外一些中国
留学生认为现在是回中国工作的好机会。为什么呢？因为21世纪以来
中国的经济发展是世界上最快的，现在是很多中国公司需要人材的时
候。加上中国留学生学习了西方的管理方式，又懂中国的文化，所以
一定会很受欢迎。我觉得这两种看法都有道理，不过我相信从西方回
中国的"海龟"肯定会越来越多。

Questions (True/False):

( ) **1.** The writer is mostly neutral regarding the two different views described.

( ) **2.** According to this passage, most Chinese students in Western countries return to China after receiving their degrees.

( ) **3.** The writer predicts that the number of Chinese students returning to China will increase.

Questions (Multiple Choice):

( ) **4.** What factors influence some Chinese students in their decision not to return to China?

　　a. higher pay and better management in Western companies

　　b. different management in Chinese companies and air pollution in some Chinese cities

　　c. environmental issues and the lack of high-level jobs in Chinese companies

( ) **5.** According to some Chinese students, why is now the best time for them to return to China?

    a. This is the time when they are most needed in Chinese companies.

    b. This is the time when the rate of economic development in China is at its fastest.

    c. This is the time when environmental pollution in China will be reduced.

( ) **6.** According to some Chinese students, what would make them welcome in Chinese companies?

    a. their foreign language abilities and knowledge of Western-style management

    b. their familiarity with both Western culture and Chinese culture

    c. their knowledge of Western-style management and familiarity with Chinese culture

2.

(TRADITIONAL)

柯林的日記

    今天是不平常的一天。下午四點，我剛下課，雪梅就給我發來短信，說她收到錄用通知了。我們太高興了，晚上我們一起去一家西餐館吃了一頓，為她的事業成功乾杯。回宿舍以後，我想了很多。我知道雪梅很喜歡那家跨國公司，她去那兒工作可不是短期打算。我很相信雪梅的能力，她在那兒一定會發展得很好。看來，她明年回美國是不太可能了。為了和雪梅在一起，我也必須考慮在北京找工作了。我的中文雖然最近進步不小，可是要在跨國企業裏工作，可能還不夠好，特別是聽力和英翻中；但是我也有優點，那就是我的專業是國際貿易，而且有實習經驗。我相信我也能找到一個適合我的工作。可是長期在中國生活，我會習慣嗎？有空的時候我要找馬克好好聊聊。他在北京生活了好幾年了，一定能給我一些好的建議。

(SIMPLIFIED)

柯林的日记

    今天是不平常的一天。下午四点，我刚下课，雪梅就给我发来短信，说她收到录用通知了。我们太高兴了，晚上我们一起去一家西餐馆吃了一顿，为她的事业成功干杯。回宿舍以后，我想了很多。我知道雪梅很喜欢那家跨国公司，她去那儿工作可不是短期打算。我很相信雪梅的能力，她在那儿一定会发展得很好。看来，她明年回美国是不太可能了。为了和雪梅在一起，我也必须考虑在北京找工作了。我的中文虽然最近进步不小，可是要在跨国企业里工作，可能还不够好，特别是听力和英翻中；但是我也有优点，那就是我的专业是国际贸易，而且有实习经验。我相信我也能找到一个适合我的工作。可是长期在中国生活，我会习惯吗？有空的时候我要找马克好好聊聊。他在北京生活了好几年了，一定能给我一些好的建议。

Questions (True/False):

( ) **1.** The company notified Xuemei via a text message that she was hired.

( ) **2.** Ke Lin and Xuemei ate at a Western-style restaurant yesterday evening.

( ) **3.** Ke Lin plans to return with Xuemei to the United States next year.

( ) **4.** Ke Lin is completely confident in his Chinese language skills.

Questions (Multiple Choice):

( ) **5.** What does Ke Lin predict for Xuemei's career in the company?

   a. She will have a long and successful career at the company.

   b. Having succeeded at the company, she will return to the United States next year.

   c. She will work there with great success and join Ke Lin at a different company later.

( ) **6.** Why does Ke Lin start thinking about finding a job in Beijing?

   a. to improve his Chinese

   b. to put his knowledge of international trade to use

   c. to be with Xuemei

( ) **7.** How does Ke Lin feel about being in Beijing for a long time?

   a. He is confident about his chances of finding a job, but not so sure about adapting to living in Beijing long-term.

   b. He is confident about his chances of finding a job and about adapting to living in Beijing long-term.

   c. He is unsure about his chances of finding a job and his ability to adapt to long-term living in Beijing.

D. Look at the ad and answer the question in Chinese. (INTERPRETIVE/PRESENTATIONAL)

 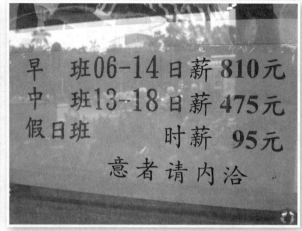

這份工作什麼時候上班薪水最高？

这份工作什么时候上班薪水最高？

E. Look at the board and answer the question. (INTERPRETIVE)

請把這個天氣預報翻譯成英文。

请把这个天气预报翻译成英文。

F.

<table>
<tr><td colspan="2" align="center">顧客意見調查表</td></tr>
<tr><td colspan="2">您是否第一次在這裏消費？
□ 是　　　　　□ 不是</td></tr>
<tr><td colspan="2">服務生是否親切的歡迎？
□ 是　　　　　□ 不是</td></tr>
<tr><td colspan="2">服務生是否主動向您推薦飲料或餐點？
□ 是　　　　　□ 不是</td></tr>
<tr><td colspan="2">服務生是否主動詢問您對我們的服務是否滿意？
□ 是　　　　　□ 不是</td></tr>
<tr><td colspan="2">服務生是否主動向您推薦飲料續杯？
□ 是　　　　　□ 不是</td></tr>
<tr><td colspan="2">您對服務生所提供服務程度？
□ 很滿意　　□ 滿意　□ 一般　□ 不滿意</td></tr>
<tr><td colspan="2">您對整體餐飲品質的滿意程度？
□ 很滿意　　□ 滿意　□ 一般　□ 不滿意</td></tr>
</table>

顧客意見調查表

您是否第一次在這裏消費？
□ 是　　　　□ 不是

服務生是否親切的歡迎？
□ 是　　　　□ 不是

服務生是否主動向您推薦飲料或餐點？
□ 是　　　　□ 不是

服務生是否主動詢問您對我們的服務是否滿意？
□ 是　　　　□ 不是

服務生是否主動向您推薦飲料續杯？
□ 是　　　　□ 不是

您對服務生所提供服務程度？
□ 很滿意　□ 滿意　□ 一般　□ 不滿意

您對整體餐飲品質的滿意程度？
□ 很滿意　□ 滿意　□ 一般　□ 不滿意

顾客意见调查表

您是否第一次在这里消费？
□ 是　　　　□ 不是

服务生是否亲切的欢迎？
□ 是　　　　□ 不是

服务生是否主动向您推荐饮料或餐点？
□ 是　　　　□ 不是

服务生是否主动询问您对我们的服务是否满意？
□ 是　　　　□ 不是

服务生是否主动向您推荐饮料续杯？
□ 是　　　　□ 不是

您对服务生所提供服务程度？
□ 很满意　□ 满意　□ 一般　□ 不满意

您对整体餐饮品质的满意程度？
□ 很满意　□ 满意　□ 一般　□ 不满意

This is a survey form. After reading it, answer the following questions. (INTERPRETIVE)

1. Who do you think is conducting the survey and who is being surveyed?

_____

2. What is the colloquial equivalent of 是否 in this context?

_____

3. Are there any questions on the survey that you would like to answer if you were asked to participate?

_____

IV. Writing and Grammar Exercises

A. Building Characters

Form a character by combining the given components as instructed. Then write a word, a phrase, or a short sentence in which that character appears.

1. 左邊一個三點水，右邊一個"每天"的"每"，
左边一个三点水，右边一个"每天"的"每"，
是 ＿＿＿＿＿＿＿＿ 的 ＿＿＿＿＿ 。

2. 左邊一個衣字旁，右邊一個"包括"的"包"，
左边一个衣字旁，右边一个"包括"的"包"，
是 ＿＿＿＿＿＿＿＿ 的 ＿＿＿＿＿ 。

3. 外邊一個"口"，裏邊一個"大小"的"大"，

　　外边一个"口"，里边一个"大小"的"大"，

　　是 ＿＿＿＿＿＿＿＿＿的＿＿＿＿＿ 。

4. 上邊一個"隹"，下邊一個"口"，

　　上边一个"隹"，下边一个"口"，

　　是 ＿＿＿＿＿＿＿＿＿的＿＿＿＿＿ 。

5. 左邊一個提手旁，右邊一個"屋子"的"屋"，

　　左边一个提手旁，右边一个"屋子"的"屋"，

　　是 ＿＿＿＿＿＿＿＿＿的＿＿＿＿＿ 。

B. First, match the full form on the left with its abbreviation on the right.

1. 國際貿易/国际贸易	**a.** 國企/国企
2. 環境保護/环境保护	**b.** 海歸/海归
3. 節約能源/节约能源	**c.** 國貿/国贸
4. 海外歸來/海外归来	**d.** 電郵/电邮
5. 國營企業/国营企业	**e.** 絲路/丝路
6. 科學技術/科学技术	**f.** 節能/节能
7. 電子郵件/电子邮件	**g.** 科技
8. 絲綢之路/丝绸之路	**h.** 環保/环保

Then, state how they relate by using 叫做, and translate the Chinese term into English.

EXAMPLE: "海外歸來"也叫做"海歸"，英文翻譯成"returning from overseas."

"海外归来"也叫做"海归"，英文翻译成"returning from overseas."

1. ＿＿＿＿＿＿＿＿＿＿＿＿＿＿＿＿＿＿＿＿＿＿＿＿＿＿＿＿＿ 。

2. ＿＿＿＿＿＿＿＿＿＿＿＿＿＿＿＿＿＿＿＿＿＿＿＿＿＿＿＿＿ 。

3. ＿＿＿＿＿＿＿＿＿＿＿＿＿＿＿＿＿＿＿＿＿＿＿＿＿＿＿＿＿ 。

4. _____ 。

5. _____ 。

6. _____ 。

7. _____ 。

C. Complete the following mini-dialogues using 又.

EXAMPLE: **A:** 這是我送給你的蛋糕。(not my birthday)

這是我送给你的蛋糕。

B: <u>今天又不是我的生日</u>，你幹嗎送我蛋糕?

<u>今天又不是我的生日</u>，你干吗送我蛋糕?

1. **A:** 你借點錢給我，行嗎? 我想投資。(have no money)

你借点钱给我，行吗? 我想投资。

B: _____，怎麼借錢給你?

_____，怎么借钱给你?

2. **A:** 這件旗袍又漂亮又便宜，買吧!　(don't wear *qipao*)

这件旗袍又漂亮又便宜，买吧!

B: _____，買了是浪費。

_____，买了是浪费。

3. **A:** 我的毛巾濕了，給我換一條乾的。　(not a wait staff)

我的毛巾湿了，给我换一条干的。

B: _____，要換自己換。

_____，要换自己换。

D. Based on common sense, state what the most desirable situation is by using "越…越…."

EXAMPLE: rent

→ 房租越便宜越好。

1. Sichuanese cuisine

→ _____。

2. salary

→ _____。

3. pressure at work

→ _____。

4. air (you breathe)

→ _____。

5. bank interest

→ _____。

E. Complete the following mini-dialogues using 既然.

EXAMPLE: **A:** 你自己去看電影吧，我累了，想回家。
你自己去看电影吧，我累了，想回家。

B: 既然你想回家，我也回家吧。

1. A: 我想投資股市，可是我沒錢。
我想投资股市，可是我没钱。

B: _____，幹嗎投資股市？
_____，干吗投资股市？

2. A: 我有點兒想搬到城裏去住，但城裏空氣污染挺嚴重的。
我有点儿想搬到城里去住，但城里空气污染挺严重的。

B: _____，就別搬了吧！

3. A: 剛才那位張先生面試的表現，我很滿意。

剛才那位张先生面试的表现，我很满意。

B: _____，就通知他下星期來上班。

_____，就通知他下星期来上班。

F. Complete the following mini-dialogues, using 好在 to introduce all the good decisions your family has made.

EXAMPLE: **A:** 最近全世界在鬧能源危機。(solar power)

最近全世界在闹能源危机。

B: 好在我們家利用太陽能發電。

好在我们家利用太阳能发电。

1. A: 最近很多人炒股賠了很多錢。(money in the bank)

最近很多人炒股赔了很多钱。

B: _____。

2. A: 醫生説熬夜對身體不好。(never do it)

医生说熬夜对身体不好。

B: _____。

3. A: 科學家説少吃肉，多吃青菜、水果有益於身體健康。(vegetarian)

科学家说少吃肉，多吃青菜、水果有益于身体健康。

B: _____。

G. First, match each person with his or her specialty.

1. 林雪梅	a. 網絡設計/网络设计
2. 雪梅的舅媽/雪梅的舅妈	b. 理財/理财
3. 總經理/总经理	c. 銷售/销售
4. 張天明/张天明	d. 投資/投资
5. 天明表哥	e. 管理

Then, state his or her specialty in a sentence.

EXAMPLE: 雪梅的舅媽善於投資，是投資方面的優秀人材。

雪梅的舅妈善于投资，是投资方面的优秀人材。

1. _____ 。

2. _____ 。

3. _____ 。

4. _____ 。

H. Translate the following dialogues into Chinese. (PRESENTATIONAL)

1. **A:** What are you looking for on the internet?

   B: I'm looking for job information.

   A: What area do you want to work in?

   B: I'd like to find something to do with environmental protection. I'm very interested in this solar energy company.

   A: Is that a multinational company? You are not only good at researching and developing new technologies, but are also familiar with Chinese and Western cultures. They will definitely welcome a "sea turtle" like you.

   _____

   _____

   _____

   _____

   _____

2. A: Can you tell me why you want to apply for this job?

   B: I majored in environmental studies in college. Besides, solar energy is inexhaustible *and* it doesn't pollute the environment. It's good for protecting the environment.

   A: Do you have work experience?

   B: I interned at an American solar energy company for six months.

   A: Do you plan to work in China on a short-term basis?

   B: No, I was born and grew up in China, and my parents are in China. That's why I plan to work in China for a long time (長期/长期).

   A: Great. Please wait for our notification.

_____

_____

_____

_____

_____

_____

_____

3. A: What do you think of the person who came for the interview today?

   B: I think she is great; she has a lot of strengths. Both her Chinese and English are good. Besides, she has internship experience in the United States.

   A: But she has one shortcoming. She doesn't have any experience in international sales.

   B: She just graduated from college, so it's unlikely for her to have a lot of experience in sales. From the way she answered questions, she seemed very intelligent. Besides, her major in college was environmental studies. I believe that she has the ability to explain (introduce) our products clearly to our customers (客戶).

   A: That makes sense. Then let's hire her.

_____

_____

_____

_____

_____

4. A: Tomorrow you'll start working at the company. You must arrange your time scientifically. Besides working, you have to pay attention to rest. Don't stay up late. Learn from others' strengths.

A: Mom, don't worry. I know. I am really not a little kid.

B: Since you know, I won't say it any more. Otherwise, the more I say, the more unhappy you are.

_____

_____

_____

_____

_____

_____

I. Translate the following passage into Chinese. (PRESENTATIONAL)

1. We are a multinational "green" beverage company. Currently, we need a sales manager. Applicants (申請者/申请者) must be good at sales and have good Chinese and English. Those who have overseas work or sales experience and understand technology are even better. This job is open to male and female applicants. Our company is for gender equality and equal work and equal pay.

_____

_____

_____

_____

_____

2. My interview today went smoothly. The manager asked me to talk about the good and bad aspects of their products. Luckily I prepared well, and the more I explained the more pleased the manager was. Before I went into his office, everyone told me the manager was stern and even scary, but as long as you answered his questions right, he was not that scary. He even shook my hand when the interview ended and told me to go home and wait for the good news.

_____

_____

_____

_____

_____

_____

J. It's important to know yourself well before you can plan your career. Write a paragraph assessing your personality, education, interests, preferences, expertise, strengths, and weaknesses. Then conclude what type of job may be a good fit for you. (PRESENTATIONAL)

K. Storytelling (PRESENTATIONAL)

Write a story in Chinese based on the four cartoons below. Make sure that your story has a beginning, a middle, and an end. Also make sure that the transition from one picture to the next is smooth and logical.

1

2

3

4

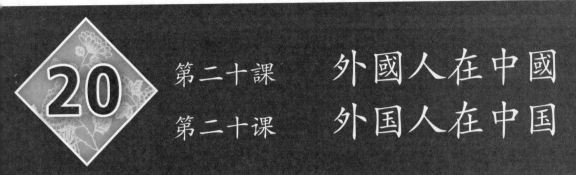

I. Listening Comprehension

A. Textbook Content (INTERPRETIVE)

Listen to the recording for the Textbook and answer the questions in English.

1. Who is attending the party, and why does this party mean different things to different people?

_____

2. What will be Xuemei's first business trip after she starts working at the company?

_____

3. Why has Li Zhe arrived in Beijing? Why does Xuemei sound particularly excited about it?

_____

4. How would you describe Mark's life in China?

_____

5. Has Lisa found it difficult to adapt to life in Beijing? Why or why not?

_____

6. Why does Li Wen say that the world has become smaller?

_____

B. Workbook Dialogue (INTERPRETIVE)

Listen to the recording for the Workbook and answer the questions.

Questions (True/False):

( ) **1.** The woman is the general manager of the company.

( ) **2.** Li Zhe will work in the sales department for three months and then be transferred to another department.

( ) **3.** The general manager will discuss Li Zhe's work with Lin Xuemei.

( ) **4.** Lin Xuemei will be Li Zhe's supervisor.

( ) **5.** Before seeing Li Zhe, the woman knew that he went to the same American university as Lin Xuemei.

C. Workbook Narratives (INTERPRETIVE)

Listen to the recording for the Workbook and answer the questions in English.

1. Questions:

a. Who is Zhang Hong? What is the purpose of this voice message?

_____

b. Who will be leaving soon, and where is she going?

_____

c. What are the two purposes of the gathering?

_____

2. Questions:

a. Who is the speaker, and who is he speaking to?

_____

b. What does the speaker call Li Xin?

_____

c. How would you describe the speaker's life in the last two days?

_____

D. Workbook Listening Rejoinder (INTERPERSONAL)

In this section, you will hear two people talking. After hearing the first speaker, select the best from the four possible responses given by the second speaker.

_____

II. Speaking Exercises

A. Practice asking and answering the following questions. (INTERPERSONAL)

1. 在一個為人接風的聚會上，説些什麼話比較合適？
   在一个为人接风的聚会上，说些什么话比较合适？

2. 在一個給人餞行的聚會上，説些什麼話比較合適？
   在一个给人饯行的聚会上，说些什么话比较合适？

3. 如果你去中國，你覺得你能不能很快地適應那兒的生活？請解釋。
   如果你去中国，你觉得你能不能很快地适应那儿的生活？请解释。

B. Practice speaking on the following topics. (PRESENTATIONAL)

1. 請談談去國外留學或生活有什麼好處。

請谈谈去国外留学或生活有什么好处。

2. 請談談去國外留學或生活以前應該有什麼樣的準備。

请谈谈去国外留学或生活以前应该有什么样的准备。

3. Predict your ability to adapt to life in China. Explain which would take you the longest to get used to—food, weather, air quality, social life, study habits, or work routine.

III. Reading Comprehension

A. Building Words

Complete this section by writing the characters, the *pinyin*, and the English equivalent of each new word formed. Guess the meaning before you use a dictionary to confirm.

1. "聚會" 的 "聚" + "晚餐" 的 "餐"

"聚会" 的 "聚" + "晚餐" 的 "餐"

→ _____ _____ _____

              new word   *pinyin*   English

2. "慶祝" 的 "慶" + "成功" 的 "功"

"庆祝" 的 "庆" + "成功" 的 "功"

→ _____ _____ _____

3. "熱水器" 的 "器" + "材料" 的 "材"

"热水器" 的 "器" + "材料" 的 "材"

→ _____ _____ _____

4. "電視劇" 的 "劇" + "書本" 的 "本"

"电视剧" 的 "剧" + "书本" 的 "本"

→ _____ _____ _____

5. "聽音樂" 的 "聽" + "眾人" 的 "眾"

"听音乐" 的 "听" + "众人" 的 "众"

→ _____ _____ _____

B. 者, 員/员 and 家 all can refer to people. Translate into English the kind of people each of the terms below refers to.

1. 者

> **a.** 讀者/读者: _____
>
> **b.** 作者: _____
>
> **c.** 老者: _____
>
> **d.** 教育工作者: _____
>
> **e.** 學者/学者: _____

2. 員/员

> **a.** 服務員/服务员: _____
>
> **b.** 售貨員/售货员: _____
>
> **c.** 運動員/运动员: _____
>
> **d.** 隊員/队员: _____
>
> **e.** 演員/演员: _____

3. 家

> **a.** 哲學家/哲学家: _____
>
> **b.** 科學家/科学家: _____
>
> **c.** 經濟學家/经济学家: _____
>
> **d.** 發明家/发明家: _____
>
> **e.** 教育家: _____
>
> **f.** 思想家: _____

C. Read the passages and answer the questions. (INTERPRETIVE)

1.

(TRADITIONAL)

　　上個星期我在一家超市看到一位年輕的西方人，覺得很面熟，一想，原來就是剛看過的電視劇裏的演員！我跟他聊了幾句，就很快地成了朋友。他來自法國，是前年冬天來中國的，所以中文名字叫冬華。冬華來中國是為了學中文，週末也當法文家教。他教七八個學生，其中有個孩子的父親是個挺有名的演員。有一次那個孩子的父親正在拍一個電視劇，劇裏邊有位年輕的外國律師，找不到合適的人演，他想到了冬華，於是就介紹他去試試。冬華沒學過表演，一開始很緊張，可是很快就適應了，大家對他都很滿意。後來，冬華又在另外兩個電視劇裏出現過，成了一位演員。

(SIMPLIFIED)

　　上个星期我在一家超市看到一位年轻的西方人，觉得很面熟，一想，原来就是刚看过的电视剧里的演员！我跟他聊了几句，就很快地成了朋友。他来自法国，是前年冬天来中国的，所以中文名字叫冬华。冬华来中国是为了学中文，周末也当法文家教。他教七八个学生，其中有个孩子的父亲是个挺有名的演员。有一次那个孩子的父亲正在拍一个电视剧，剧里边有位年轻的外国律师，找不到合适的人演，他想到了冬华，于是就介绍他去试试。冬华没学过表演，一开始很紧张，可是很快就适应了，大家对他都很满意。后来，冬华又在另外两个电视剧里出现过，成了一位演员。

Questions (True/False):

( ) **1.** The author of this passage is an actor.

( ) **2.** Donghua received his Chinese name from his Chinese teacher in France.

( ) **3.** The writer and Donghua have been friends for about two years.

( ) **4.** Donghua has performed in three TV dramas so far.

Questions (Multiple Choice):

( ) **5.** Which of the following is true about Donghua's tutoring?

    a. One of his students was a famous actor.

    b. One of his students had a son who was a famous actor.

    c. One of his students had a father who was a famous actor.

( ) **6.** Which of the following is true about Donghua's performance in his first TV drama?

    a. He quickly overcame his initial nervousness, despite his lack of acting experience.

    b. He succeeded even though his lack of acting experience initially made the director nervous.

    c. His role of a language tutor satisfied the director and the people around him.

2.

(TRADITIONAL)

在中國長期生活的外國人主要有兩種。第一種人很多，他們在大學當教授或者在公司裏當管理人員，有固定的工作，收入都比較高。這種人雖然工作也會有壓力，但是生活一般都很舒服。另外一種人是自由職業者，他們有時候當翻譯，有時候做家教，有時候當導遊，有時候甚至當演員。這種人因為有時有工作，有時沒工作，所以收入不太穩定。但是由於中國的東西一般都比較便宜，所以他們的生活還是沒問題的。更重要的是，他們能認識很多中國一般百姓，交很多朋友，所以比教授和管理人員更容易融入中國社會。在這兩種外國人中，第二種人雖然賺錢比較少，可是他們往往比第一種人更了解中國的生活。

(SIMPLIFIED)

在中国长期生活的外国人主要有两种。第一种人很多，他们在大学当教授或者在公司里当管理人员，有固定的工作，收入都比较高。这种人虽然工作也会有压力，但是生活一般都很舒服。另外一种人是自由职业者，他们有时候当翻译，有时候做家教，有时候当导游，有时候甚至当演员。这种人因为有时有工作，有时没工作，所以收入不太稳定。但是由于中国的东西一般都比较便宜，所以他们的生活还是没问题的。更重要的是，他们能认识很多中国一般百姓，交很多朋友，所以比教授和管理人员更容易融入中国社会。在这两种外国人中，第二种人虽然赚钱比较少，可是他们往往比第一种人更了解中国的生活。

Questions (True/False):

( ) **1.** This passage is about how to find jobs in China.

( ) **2.** According to the passage, foreigners in China who have a stable income usually live a stress-free life.

( ) **3.** Foreigners who are freelance professionals in China often have to live on the fringe of Chinese society.

Questions (Multiple Choice):

( ) **4.** According to the passage, foreigners who are freelance professionals in China often work as _____.

   a. managers, translators, tutors, and actors

   b. translators, professors, actors, and tour guides

   c. tutors, tour guides, actors, and translators

D. Look at the blackboard and answer the question in English. (INTERPRETIVE)

Who's needed? _____

E. Look at the ad and answer the question in English. (INTERPRETIVE)

這是什麼廣告？他們賣什麼？請用英文寫出兩樣。

这是什么广告？他们卖什么？请用英文写出两样。

IV. Writing and Grammar Exercises

A. Building Characters

Form a character by combining the given components as instructed. Then write a word, a phrase, or a short sentence in which that character appears.

1. 左邊一個 "小區" 的 "區"，右邊一個 "欠錢" 的 "欠"，
　　左边一个 "小区" 的 "区"，右边一个 "欠钱" 的 "欠"，
　　是 ＿＿＿＿＿＿＿ 的 ＿＿＿＿ 。

2. 左邊一個提手旁，右邊一個 "高樓" 的 "高"，
　　左边一个提手旁，右边一个 "高楼" 的 "高"，
　　是 ＿＿＿＿＿＿＿ 的 ＿＿＿＿ 。

3. 左邊一個 "木"，右邊一個 "交通" 的 "交"，
　　左边一个 "木"，右边一个 "交通" 的 "交"，
　　是 ＿＿＿＿＿＿＿ 的 ＿＿＿＿ 。

4. 左邊一個人字旁，右邊一個 "一直" 的 "直"，
　　左边一个人字旁，右边一个 "一直" 的 "直"，
　　是 ＿＿＿＿＿＿＿ 的 ＿＿＿＿ 。

5. 左邊一個言字旁，右邊一個 "便宜" 的 "宜"，
　　左边一个言字旁，右边一个 "便宜" 的 "宜"，
　　是 ＿＿＿＿＿＿＿ 的 ＿＿＿＿ 。

B. Using 把, list the possibilities for managing one's money.

1. depositing it in the bank

→ _____

2. investing it in the stock market

→ _____

3. giving it to your parents

→ _____

4. lending it to your classmate

→ _____

5. placing it under your pillow

→ _____

6. placing it under your bed

→ _____

7. spending it all

→ _____

C. Suppose you are planning for a welcoming or farewell party. First, list all the tasks.

1. _____   **5.** _____

2. _____   **6.** _____

3. _____   **7.** _____

4. _____   **8.** _____

Second, designate who's responsible for which task.

1. (Item listed in #1) 由 (classmate's name) V。

2. _____

3. _____

4. _____

5. _____

6._____

7._____

8._____

D. Complete the following mini-dialogues using 而已 to understate the answers.

EXAMPLE: **A:** 聽説你炒股，賠了一些錢。

听说你炒股，赔了一些钱。
(two hundred)

→ **B:** 不多，<u>只賠了兩百塊錢而已</u>。

不多，<u>只赔了两百块钱而已</u>。

1. **A:** 看你買這麼多菜，今天晚上你請幾個人來吃火鍋?

看你买这么多菜，今天晚上你请几个人来吃火锅?
(five people)

→ **B:** 別緊張，_____。

別緊张，_____。

2. **A:** 你一會兒搞翻譯，一會兒搞推銷，一會兒又當家教，你到底有幾份工作啊? 不累啊?

你一会儿搞翻译，一会儿搞推销，一会儿又当家教，你到底有几份工作啊? 不累啊?
(three jobs)

→ **B:** 不累，_____。

不累，_____。

3. **A:** 你對這個城市這麼熟悉，看來，在這兒已經待了很長一段時間了。

你对这个城市这么熟悉，看来，在这儿已经待了很长一段时间了。
(half a year)

→ **B:** 不長，_____。

不长，_____。

E. Translate the following sentences into Chinese using 在⋯下.(PRESENTATIONAL)

1. With colleagues' help, he got used to his new job very quickly.

_____

2. Under the instruction (教育) of his professor, he got his master's degree without a hitch.

_____

3. Persuaded by his parents, he decided not to invest in the stock market.

_____

F. Translate the following dialogues into Chinese. (PRESENTATIONAL)

1. A: Thank you for your help. If it weren't for your contacting that TV station, they wouldn't have let me act in that TV drama.

B: I was simply making a phone call. It's not worth mentioning.

_____

_____

_____

2. A: How was the sales situation of the water heaters last month?

B: What do you think? Under your leadership, we have become one of the three biggest water heater companies in the world. The more we market and promote our products, the more our sales thrive.

A: Wonderful. We should get together tonight to celebrate.

B: I'm all for it. (I raise both hands to support this proposal.)

_____

_____

_____

_____

_____

G. Translate the following passages into Chinese. (PRESENTATIONAL)

1. Classmates, thank you for hosting this farewell dinner for me. Who knew that four years of college life would go by so quickly? Tomorrow I'll fly back to Mexico. When I came to China, I didn't know a word of Chinese. Because everyone often helped and took care of me, I've lived these four years in China in great happiness. Every day I see and hear something new. I'll never forget (all these things). I also have to thank Teacher Bai for teaching me many things. Come, I wish everyone health and a successful career.

_____

_____

_____

_____

_____

_____

_____

2. Pepe (裴佩) and I were roommates for four years, so I have to say a few words. The school asked me to help Pepe learn Chinese, but I felt that I've learned a lot of things from Pepe. Pepe is a soccer fan. The reason I am so healthy today is because no matter how busy we were with schoolwork (學習/学习), every weekend Pepe made me go to the soccer field with him to play soccer. He made me realize that heath and academics are equally important. I'll never forget you, Pepe. Now let's invite Teacher Bai to say a few words.

_____

_____

_____

_____

_____

_____

_____

3. Pepe (裴佩), I want to first congratulate you on finding a great job. Has Pepe told everyone that he's found a job with a Chinese company in Mexico? I heard that Pepe wasn't nervous at all at the interview. He performed very well. The manager who interviewed him felt that Pepe was very capable and had a lot of strengths. I'm really happy for him. Pepe, I wish you a safe journey tomorrow and a successful career.

_____

_____

_____

_____

_____

4. Today was my first day at work. Next month I'll go to Europe on a business trip to promote our company's solar water heaters. Our company's products are excellent in quality but affordable in price. Besides, they are good for the environment, so they sell extremely well. I have three schoolmates in our company. They said they would take care of me. I'll call my mom this weekend to tell her that my work will go without a hitch and ask her to stop worrying.

_____

_____

_____

_____

_____

5. My schoolmate Wang Ziming (王子明) has been working at the company for three years after graduating from college. He says that although the work is very interesting, there is also a lot of pressure. Sometimes he has to stay up late. He is really quite impressive, having become manager of the international sales department at such a young age. Not only does he understand sales, but he is also an outstanding manager. The only thing is that I think he needs to pay more attention to rest. I hope he can go on a tour occasionally to relax a little bit.

_____

_____

_____

_____

_____

_____

_____

H. A classmate in your Chinese class is graduating at the end of the semester. What would you write on a graduation card or a banner for a send-off party to wish him or her great success in the future? (PRESENTATIONAL)

I. You've known the characters of the textbook for many months. Create a personal bio of one of your favorite or least favorite characters. Include basic information about his or her upbringing, hobbies, interests, personality, education, work experience, future aspirations, flaws, strengths, etc. Make sure to explain why you like or dislike him or her, and if you wish, whether you and the character are alike in any way. (PRESENTATIONAL)

J. Storytelling (PRESENTATIONAL)

Write a story in Chinese based on the four cartoons below. Make sure that your story has a beginning, a middle, and an end. Also make sure that the transition from one picture to the next is smooth and logical.

1

2

3

4

Let's Review (LESSONS 16–20)

I. How Good Is Your Pronunciation?

Write down the correct pronunciation and tones of the following short sentences in *pinyin*, and use a recording device or computer to record them. Hand in the recording to your teacher if asked. Then translate each sentence into English. (INTERPRETIVE)

1. 新鮮、不受污染的空氣有益於身體健康。

新鲜、不受污染的空气有益于身体健康。

_____

_____

2. 風能是大自然取之不盡的能源之一。

风能是大自然取之不尽的能源之一。

_____

_____

3. 政府規定，夏天公共場所的空調溫度不可低於攝氏26度。

政府规定，夏天公共场所的空调温度不可低于摄氏26度。

_____

_____

4. 很多退休老人把自己省吃儉用攢下來的錢，拿去投資風險較大的股市。

很多退休老人把自己省吃俭用攒下来的钱，拿去投资风险较大的股市。

_____

_____

5. 最近世界的經濟危機，引起很多人對自己的理財方式進行思考。
最近世界的经济危机，引起很多人对自己的理财方式进行思考。

---

6. 他終於說服妻子把存款從銀行拿出來，小兩口決定要好好消
費，好好享受生活。
他终于说服妻子把存款从银行拿出来，小两口决定要好好消
费，好好享受生活。

---

7. "有朋自遠方來，不亦樂乎"，這句話有兩千多年的歷史。
"有朋自远方来，不亦乐乎"，这句话有两千多年的历史。

---

8. 秦始皇對中國文字的統一有貢獻，但他修墳墓、修宮殿、殺讀
書人、燒古書，也引起老百姓對他的不滿。
秦始皇对中国文字的统一有贡献，但他修坟墓、修宫殿、杀读
书人、烧古书，也引起老百姓对他的不满。

---

9. 中國歷史非常長，曾經是科技發達，技術先進的文明古國。
中国历史非常长，曾经是科技发达，技术先进的文明古国。

---

10. 他學有所成，從海外歸來，今天去某家跨國公司面試。他對自
己的表現很不滿意，覺得十分鬱悶。
他学有所成，从海外归来，今天去某家跨国公司面试。他对自
己的表现很不满意，觉得十分郁闷。

11. 那位總經理雖然有些嚴肅，但的確是管理方面的優秀人材。
那位总经理虽然有些严肃，但的确是管理方面的优秀人材。

_____

_____

12. 收到錄用通知時，他的臉上馬上多雲轉晴，笑了起來。
收到录用通知时，他的脸上马上多云转晴，笑了起来。

_____

_____

13. 每週工作聚會時，他都希望經理、同事告訴他自己的優缺點。
每周工作聚会时，他都希望经理、同事告诉他自己的优缺点。

_____

_____

14. 這位演員不僅年輕、漂亮，而且善於推銷新産品，很多公司都找
她拍廣告，最近特別火。
这位演员不仅年轻、漂亮，而且善于推销新产品，很多公司都找
她拍广告，最近特别火。

_____

_____

15. 他要移民去歐洲，朋友們給他餞行，大家為友誼乾杯，並互祝身
體健康，生活幸福，事業成功。
他要移民去欧洲，朋友们给他饯行，大家为友谊干杯，并互祝身
体健康，生活幸福，事业成功。

_____

_____

II. Put Your Chinese to Good Use! (PRESENTATIONAL)

Imagine that you are going to China. Before you go, find out if you know enough Chinese to talk about some interesting topics:

A. Suppose you want to share your knowledge about how people conserve energy and protect the environment in your own country. What would you say?

節能/节能

環保/环保

_____

_____

_____

_____

_____

_____

_____

_____

_____

_____

_____

_____

B. Suppose you want to share some basic strategies for financial planning and investment. What would you suggest?

理財/理财

投資/投资

_____

_____

_____

_____

_____

_____

_____

_____

_____

_____

C. Suppose you want to demonstrate your knowledge of Chinese history. What dynasties or historical figures would you mention and what would you say about the roles those historical figures played?

朝代 歷史人物／历史人物

————————————————   ————————————————

————————————————   ————————————————

————————————————   ————————————————

————————————————   ————————————————

D. Suppose you are talking with your new friends about why you have come to China and how you see yourself adapting to life in China. What sorts of things would you mention?

什麼吸引你來中國留學/工作？　什么吸引你来中国留学/工作？

————————————————————————————————

————————————————————————————————

————————————————————————————————

————————————————————————————————

你怎麼能很快地適應中國　你怎么能很快地适应中国
的生活？　的生活？

————————————————————————————————

————————————————————————————————

————————————————————————————————

————————————————————————————————

E. Suppose you are planning to see off a Chinese friend who is going to work in your country and welcome someone from your country who has just arrived in China to study Chinese. What wishes would you express for each occasion?

餞行/饯行　　　　　　　　接風/接风

_____　　_____

_____　　_____

_____　　_____

III. Getting to Know Yourself! (PRESENTATIONAL)

A. Describe three things that you can do daily to save energy and reduce your carbon footprint, with #1 as the most frequently done.

1. _____

2. _____

3. _____

B. Describe three good practices that will help you achieve your financial goals, with #1 as the least risky and most helpful.

1. _____

2. _____

3. _____

C. Describe three things that you think can make a good impression on the interviewer when you are being interviewed for a job, with #1 as most important.

1. _____

2. _____

3. _____

D. Describe three Chinese historical events that are impressive to you, with #1 as the most impressive.

1. _____

2. _____

3. _____

Explain why they interest you.

E. Come up with three questions that you would ask a friend who has lived in China about his or her adaptation to life in China, with #1 as the most important.

1. _____

2. _____

3. _____

IV. Express Yourself! (INTERPERSONAL AND PRESENTATIONAL)

Interview your Chinese teacher and students from China on campus to ask for their advice for students like you who wish to study or work in China. Organize your notes and write a simple report based on your interviews.

Include advice on food, housing, commuting, budgeting, shopping, internship and job opportunities, and some basic essential facts about Chinese geography and history.